Sheldon s
(

Dr Cheryl Rezek is a consultant clinical psychologist and mindfulness teacher who brings a fresh and dynamic approach to how mindfulness and psychological concepts can be integrated into everyone's life as a way of managing it in the most helpful way. Her work is engaging, accessible and, most importantly, realistic, and her writing easy to read and follow, giving it a broad appeal to all audiences. Her model (affectionately known as Life Happens) is based on academic knowledge and her extensive clinical experience, and it is regarded as an emerging mindfulness-based approach. It encourages awareness of oneself within a context, the development of resilience and skills, and the use of mindfulness. She has a long-standing clinical and academic career; she's lectured, supervised, developed programmes, appeared on radio and TV shows, as well as run workshops nationally and internationally. She is the author of a number of books, including *Life Happens: Waking up to yourself and your life in a mindful way* (Leachcroft); *Mindfulness: How the mindful approach can help you towards a better life* (Pearson); *Mindfulness for Carers: How to manage the demands of caregiving while finding a place for yourself* (Jessica Kingsley); *Monkey Mind and the Mountain: Mindfulness for 8–12-year-olds (and older)* (Leachcroft); and *Sheldon Mindfulness: Anxiety and Depression* (Sheldon Press). Dr Rezek also has a highly rated app entitled *iMindfulness on the Go* (Android and iOS).

Visit her website at <www.lifehappens-mindfulness.com>.

D0313651

Sheldon Mindfulness

Selected titles

A full list of titles is available from Sheldon Press,
36 Causton Street, London SW1P 4ST and on our website at
www.sheldonpress.co.uk

Anxiety and Depression
Dr Cheryl Rezek

Quit Smoking
Dr Cheryl Rezek

Compassion
Caroline Latham

Stress
Philip Cowell and Lorraine Millard

Keeping a Journal
Philip Cowell

Sheldon Mindfulness

Quit Smoking

DR CHERYL REZEK

First published in Great Britain in 2016

Sheldon Press
36 Causton Street
London SW1P 4ST
www.sheldonpress.co.uk

British Library Cataloguing-in-Publication Data
A catalogue record for this book is available from the British Library

ISBN 978-1-84709-419-3
eBook ISBN 978-1-84709-420-9

Typeset by Fakenham Prepress Solutions, Fakenham, Norfolk NR21 8NN
First printed in Great Britain by Ashford Colour Press
Subsequently digitally reprinted in Great Britain

eBook by Fakenham Prepress Solutions, Fakenham, Norfolk NR21 8NN

Produced on paper from sustainable forests

Thank you to Tom Davey for his help with this project.

Contents

An important note about the text

To access the audio downloads that accompany this book, go to: <www.lifehappens-mindfulness.com/book-audio>.

Do not listen to the audio download material while driving or operating any machinery or item.

Disclaimer: This book makes no claim to act as a cure or treatment of any conditions, nor does it advocate discontinuation of any intervention or treatment.

Introduction

Life Happens

Life is not a simple existence but more of a curiously complex experience. Many of us will have felt at some stage that life is going faster than we can keep up with it. What this book will provide are suggestions as to how you can discover calm amid what may feel like chaos. Putting mindfulness into practice will supply the groundwork for you to acquire a greater degree of stability and choice in how you live your life without smoking.

Life happens to all of us. Sometimes it is good or wonderful and other times decidedly awful. No matter what, we have a choice on our view of life and how to respond to situations in which we find ourselves, even when they are challenging.

We all know that there can be difficult situations in life, whether physical or psychological. When the downs are experienced, smoking can be used as a coping method to manage stress, pain or anxieties. The trouble is that smoking is often enjoyable, so who wants to give up something that is pleasurable, even if it's harmful? Some of you may feel as though smoking is the only way you are able to relax. Mindfulness can be useful if you are looking for an alternative to smoking that can help you develop a healthier management of your behaviour and life or if you're stressed, tense or anxious. It's also for those who realize smoking is an addiction and want to stop.

What use could this book be for me?

Reading through this book will introduce you to the concept of mindfulness and how it can be applied to help you kick the smoking habit and control your thoughts and emotions in a more balanced, accepting way. A summary of the history of mindfulness will be presented, as well as of research that has been published on how mindfulness can specifically aid people who smoke and how it also helps in other areas.

Throughout the book there are practices for you to use and assistance with doing these through step-by-step guides.

> To download the guided meditations, go to <www.lifehappens-mindfulness/book-audio>. Whenever you see this symbol 🔊 it indicates that there is a guided meditation in the form of an audio download that you can listen to.

Try all the written practices as well as those on the audio download *at least once*. You will then get to know which practices work best for you. Do these practices frequently enough for them to have a positive impact over the future days, weeks and even years. If practised enough, mindfulness can offer you support and strength in your resolve to stop smoking, both now and in the future. Realistically though, it can only help if you do the practices on a fairly regular basis and if you at least try to integrate the mindset of mindfulness into your life.

There is no magic wand but there is a solution.

The truth of it

Here are a few things that need stating before you start.

- You don't need facts and figures on the percentage of people who do or don't develop illnesses or die from smoking – you know how harmful it is.

- The art of self-deception alternates with guilt and fear in addictions.
- We play games with ourselves and put up barriers to avoid doing what needs to be done – 'I'm too busy'; 'This stuff is silly'; 'I'll take my chances'. You've said it all before and others have heard it all before.
- Addictions are addictions but that doesn't mean you have no control over them.
- If you really want to stop smoking, you will, no matter how hard it is.
- If you want to stop you need to make this personal. This is about your life, and if you quit smoking it needs to be because you want to do it at a gut level, for yourself, not for anyone else.
- If you're stopping smoking, or any other addiction, for someone else then you're trying to make them responsible for your life.
- You are your responsibility – not your family's, your doctor's, your children's, your boss's.
- When you take responsibility for yourself you take back control.
- You'll stop smoking long term only when you change your mindset. It's about shifting from 'I'm trying to stop smoking' to 'I don't smoke' (and all that goes with it).
- Substitutes are exactly that – they don't shift or alter your mindset, attitude, feelings or behaviours.
- You will relapse if you don't shift the attitude, behaviours and associations that come with smoking.
- If you do what you've always done, you'll get what you've always got. If you don't want to get your hand burnt then don't put it on a hot stove. There's no point in placing it there and hoping it won't get burnt – it will, the stove is hot. Make the links.
- Treat this book as stupid and pointless and that's exactly what it will be. Treat it as something of use and having a purpose and that's exactly what it will be.
- You can stop. Don't give up if you relapse. Keep at it – use things that help and you will do it. It can take up to 11 attempts before stopping on a permanent basis, so there is hope.[1]

Part 1

What is mindfulness and how can it help me?

1

Why do I smoke?

It is estimated that around 10 million people in the UK smoke[1] and approximately 1.3 billion people worldwide. Smoking is not only a behaviour but a frequently repeated behaviour that becomes a normal part of your everyday life; that is, a habit. Whether you smoke several packs a day or five cigarettes a day, it's still a habit, albeit varying in severity.

Why people smoke can be summarized as having two prime causes:

1 The physiological aspect: the most addictive ingredient of a cigarette is the stimulant nicotine, which can contrastingly have both a calming and excitatory effect.[2] It has been shown to increase heart rate, reaction time and cognitive processing of information while also calming and composing your emotions. Nicotine in a cigarette takes just ten seconds from being inhaled to reaching your brain, and it triggers the release of a chemical, dopamine, in the brain that brings sensations of pleasure. It can improve your mood and concentration, relax you, make you feel less hungry and help you feel less angry or stressed. However, over time more nicotine is required to release the same amount of dopamine[3] and the positive effects are short lived.

2 Smoking is essentially your mind's and body's logical search for a shortcut to solving a problem. That problem could be your feeling stress, anxiety or pain, for example. Instead of facing the problem,

which can often be difficult, you may turn to smoking as an avoidance technique. However, at times it may not be as complicated as that and can simply be due to your knowing smoking has brought enjoyment or pleasure in the past so you repeat the behaviour. The label of smoking as only self-destructive is a misinterpretation of what the coping process involved in the smoking behaviour is all about. For example:

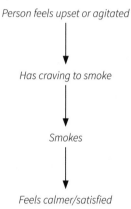

Person feels upset or agitated

Has craving to smoke

Smokes

Feels calmer/satisfied

Changes in the brain start to occur as you give it nicotine on a regular basis. When you aren't feeding the receptor sites in your brain with nicotine they react, leading you to feel agitated. You begin to crave and you satisfy it by smoking. This is then associated with pleasure or with a reduction in discomfort that is sometimes interpreted as pleasure. The nicotine reduces once again over a short time, the receptor sites become demanding, you feel a craving, smoke, and so a cycle or habit begins. This is discussed in more depth in Chapter 6 on the addiction cycle.

It is likely that at some time during this process you will feel guilt, knowing that your choice to smoke is not good for you in the long term but that the attraction of smoking is that it makes you feel better in the immediate short term. Significantly more often than not, the choice to make you feel better now will seem more enticing than the choice that will make you feel better in the years to come.

Table 1 To smoke or not to smoke

Choice 1: SMOKE	Choice 2: DON'T SMOKE
Unhealthy choice but quick resolution to problem	Healthy choice but benefits not immediate
Destructive long term but attractive short term	Unattractive short term
Familiar	Unfamiliar and requires dedication and effort to stop, particularly in the short term
Pleasurable	Unpleasant cravings

A few interesting facts

- Smoking is the single most preventable cause of death in the world.[4]
- Around 5 per cent of children under the age of 16 in the UK smoke regularly.[5]
- It can harm nearly every organ in the body and it causes nearly one of every five deaths in the USA each year.[6]
- Tobacco use kills almost 6 million people worldwide each year.[7]
- Smoking causes more deaths each year than all the following combined: human immunodeficiency virus (HIV), illegal drug use, alcohol use, motor-vehicle injuries and firearm-related incidents.[8]
- Each year, 600,000 non-smokers worldwide die from exposure to environmental tobacco smoke.[9]
- Nicotine is the most addictive element. It gives a surge of energy as it is a central nervous system stimulant, but it has both a calming and an excitatory effect.[10]
- Nicotine is as addictive as heroin or cocaine[11] and changes the brain as much as they do.[12]
- Cigarette smoke contains over 7,000 chemicals, including 70 known cancer-causing (carcinogenic) compounds and 400 other toxins, such as nicotine, tar, carbon monoxide, nitrogen oxide, formaldehyde, ammonia, benzene, cyanide, arsenic and DDT.[13]

Smoking rates among adults with depression in the UK are about twice those of adults without depression. Adolescents who misuse alcohol or drugs, have stressful environments or live in poverty are more likely to smoke, possibly due to the stress associated with these lifestyles/situations. In addition, role modelling by parents, relatives and friends, as well as parental attitudes, play a part too, as do the social influences surrounding the adolescent or adult.[14] Genetics also play an important part in smoking initiation, maintenance and dependence.[15]

Despite its temptation or enjoyment, smoking is obviously not a healthy addition to your life, and it is linked to a wide variety of physical and mental health problems.

Physical health

Problems may include:

- increased likelihood of developing many different types of cancer, including lung, mouth, throat, nose, liver, kidney, stomach, pancreatic, bladder, bowel, ovarian;
- potential lung difficulties leading to emphysema, tuberculosis and bronchitis;
- increase in blood cholesterol and more likelihood of developing chronic pulmonary diseases;
- increased likelihood of developing Alzheimer's Disease;
- increased risk of fertility or sexual conditions for both men and women, e.g. erectile disorders and impotence, folliculogenesis and risk to health of the uterus;
- health risk to the foetus in pregnant women who smoke, and increased likelihood of issues such as growth reduction, foetal asphyxiation and foetal premature deliveries;
- increased risk of gum disease;
- decrease in bone density;
- compromised immune system;
- potential effects on the brain due to the nicotine in cigarettes;

- potential effects on the entire body – the chemicals in cigarettes enter the blood stream;
- damage to the body's DNA because of these chemicals;
- possible priming or predisposing of the brain to become addicted to other substances due to nicotine, as suggested by recent research.[16]

Mental health

Problems may include:

- potential marked increase in stress levels due to long-term nicotine intake;
- unstable mood, feelings of guilt, embarrassment and shame;
- decrease in IQ and loss of memory;
- panic attacks and depression or feeling tearful;
- feelings of bitterness, anger, frustration or resent, as well as fear or helplessness.

Withdrawal

A common mistake smokers make is trying to stop altogether rather than reduce their nicotine intake over time in order to allow their bodies time to adjust. This can lead to unpleasant withdrawal symptoms, such as:

- slower heart rate
- headaches or nausea
- severe cravings
- drowsiness
- constipation
- hunger
- mood swings
- irritability or anxiety
- feelings of exhaustion or depression
- increased appetite

- insomnia or restlessness
- weight gain.

The worst withdrawal symptoms tend to be during the first seven days. Even when they are extreme, be assured that they will lessen over time and that there are no health dangers from nicotine withdrawal. In spite of such discomfort and even desperation, stopping smoking is the best thing you can do for your overall health. The health benefits of quitting far exceed any weight gains.

It should be noted too that people can become depressed or find their mood lower when they stop smoking as nicotine withdrawal can mimic symptoms of depression as well as bring about depression.[17] This is because there are adaptations that take place in the brain at a neurological level when nicotine is withdrawn.

More on smoking and mental health

Although there is a strong link between smoking and depression, there is insufficient evidence to say that one automatically causes the other – but smoking certainly does increase the risk of becoming depressed.[18,19] As previously mentioned, this occurs because nicotine has a neurobiologic impact on the brain; that is, it changes the brain and consequently may damage certain pathways in the brain that regulate mood and relate to depression. Nicotine tweaks the brain, which initially provides pleasure and regulates mood; over time, however, the brain needs increasing amounts of nicotine for the same effect. Trying to stop can then lead to anxiety and symptoms of depression, which become hard to manage so that a return to smoking is often seen as the solution. It can be a chicken-and-egg scenario whereby depression and anxiety increase the risk of smoking and smoking increases the risk of depression and anxiety, even schizophrenia.[20,21,22,23]

Depressed people are much more likely to smoke than people who aren't, and people smoke more in line with their level of depression;

that is, as they feel more depressed they smoke more.[24] The same has been found for anxiety.[25,26,27]

A large study in the USA[28] found that 48 per cent of women and 40 per cent of men with severe depression were smokers. Of those who were not depressed but smoked, 17 per cent were women and 25 per cent men. It was also found that over 50 per cent of people who were depressed smoked a cigarette within five minutes of waking but only 30 per cent who weren't depressed did this.

In general, depressed people smoke more than people who aren't depressed, and among smokers, depressed smokers smoke more than non-depressed smokers. Some research suggests that this may be due to cigarettes containing an antidepressant-like substance that may affect mood, so that people with depression may use smoking as a form of self-medication. It is also known that many people smoke to regulate feelings of restlessness, anxiety and depression. Those who experience depression may also experience more severe nicotine withdrawal and are about 40 per cent less likely to quit smoking than those smokers who aren't depressed.[29] Interestingly, people who are depressed are more likely to have tried smoking than non-depressed people.[30]

Although it is often believed that smoking reduces anxiety, the opposite is true: it has been found to increase anxiety and may actually cause it, as noted above. In research, people who successfully stopped smoking reported a considerable drop in anxiety levels compared with those who did not quit, and this was found particularly in those who used smoking to cope with stress and anxiety rather than in those who used smoking as a form of pleasure.[31]

Smoking may cause depression but depression certainly increases your chances of smoking, of smoking more and of finding it harder to stop.

People with mental health disorders have a life expectancy eight years lower than the general population, which may be due to smoking.[32]

Studies have been done with adolescents, and over an 18-month period among high-school attendees it was found that heavy smokers at the beginning of the study were more likely to grow more depressed over time than those who smoked less or not at all, and that those who had a persistent depression at the beginning were more likely to increase their smoking than whose who weren't depressed.[33] Furthermore, cigarette smoking may increase the risk of certain anxiety disorders, namely agoraphobia, generalized anxiety disorder and panic disorder, during late adolescence and early adulthood.[34]

Warning signs and symptoms of depression

The following are only indicators and not everyone will feel depressed or have all the symptoms, so it is important to have a balanced view but also to recognize that if you do have a number of these symptoms, you should seek professional help or support. Needless to say, if you have suicidal feelings or want to self-harm, you should immediately ask for assistance.

It's helpful to know that you can have a low mood or feel depressed without it needing a psychiatric diagnosis, label or medication, unless prescribed by your doctor. It's about recognizing how you feel, acknowledging it and then addressing it so that it doesn't become harmful to you. Look out for the following:

- persistent sad, anxious or low mood, including feeling empty;
- feelings of hopelessness and pessimism;
- feelings of guilt, worthlessness or helplessness;
- loss of interest or pleasure in hobbies and activities that were once enjoyed, including sex;
- decreased energy, feeling fatigued or being slowed down;
- difficulty concentrating, remembering or making decisions;
- insomnia, early-morning awakening or oversleeping;
- poor appetite, loss of interest in food, or ongoing overeating;
- thoughts of self-harm or suicide;
- restlessness, irritability and agitation, especially in men;
- risk-taking, such as dangerous driving, drinking, drugs, gambling, unprotected sex, monetary deals;

- persistent physical symptoms that don't respond to treatment, such as headaches, pain and digestive problems.

Stopping smoking can improve your mental health

Smoking doesn't make you feel better. When you're withdrawing from nicotine you feel agitated or low, so you crave; and the nicotine from the cigarette you then smoke makes you feel better, mostly because your agitation has stopped as the receptor sites in your brain have now had their fix, rather than it improving your mental health in any real way. Quitting may cause initial changes in one's mental state (for anyone), but in most cases these soon subside once past the nicotine withdrawal period.

Many individuals with mental health difficulties, as well as professionals working with them, are concerned that stopping smoking will decrease a person's mental or emotional stability and that this will lead to depression, agitation or anxiety. However, it's now being found that people with mental health disorders are not negatively affected by quitting and, in fact, they show an increase in mental health benefits. An improvement in everyone's quality of life; that is, for those with or without a mental health disorder who stop smoking, has been found.[35] Quitting smoking is as good, if not better, for improving anxiety and low mood in patients with mental health disorders than antidepressants, and it actually reduces anxiety.[36,37]

Second-hand smoke

It is worth mentioning second-hand smoke as the effects are almost as detrimental as if the other person was a smoker. Second-hand smoke has 4,000 chemicals, toxins and poisonous gases, many of which are toxic and cause cancer, damage the brain and kidneys, cause heart and respiratory diseases and cause death. It is especially harmful to pregnant women, babies and children, causing conditions such as small birth size of babies, SIDS (Sudden Infant Death

Syndrome); weak lungs, severe asthma, breathing problems, bronchitis, pneumonia and ear infections.

Second-hand smoke increases the recipient's chances of getting lung cancer by 20–30 per cent and heart disease by 25–30 per cent, and in the USA each year 3,000 people die of lung cancer and 33,000 of heart disease primarily as a result of being exposed to second-hand smoke.[38]

Smokeless tobacco

The effects of these products are often overlooked as they aren't inhaled. Their use is not common in every country but they're still actively used in places such as the USA, India, Asia and Africa.

Smokeless products include:

- chewing tobacco
- snuff
- moist snuff (dip and snus)
- dissolvable products, such as lozenges, orbs, sticks and strips.

Smokeless tobacco is harmful and has many health implications.[39]

- It contains 28 cancer-causing agents (carcinogens).
- It is known to cause cancer, particularly oral and pancreatic cancer.
- It is strongly associated with leukoplakia – a precancerous lesion of the soft tissue in the mouth that consists of a white patch or plaque that cannot be scraped off.
- It is associated with recession of the gums, gum disease and tooth decay.
- Used during pregnancy, it increases the risk for pre-eclampsia, premature birth and low birth weight.
- Used by men it causes reduced sperm count and abnormal sperm cells.
- It contains nicotine and using it leads to nicotine addiction and dependence.
- Adolescents who use it are more likely to become cigarette smokers.

The message seems clear: tobacco in any form is harmful, even if it's not smoked.

Keep trying

The good news is that some of these negative effects can be reversed or reduced when you stop smoking. By quitting, your cardiovascular risks decrease after just one year, so your risk for a heart attack drops sharply within two to five years after stopping, your risk for stroke could fall to about the same as a non-smoker's, your risks for cancers of the mouth, throat, oesophagus and bladder drop by half within five and ten years after you stop, and your risk for lung cancer drops by half in the same period.[40]

The receptor sites in the brain for nicotine reduce over a period of time and are no longer active from 2–4 weeks after quitting. However, the psychological addiction remains, which is why it is so important to address this side of your addiction and to develop your resilience and skills to counteract and manage this aspect. If you don't, the chances of relapse are greatly increased.

Mindfulness practice: The Shower

When you are in the shower or bath, become aware of the water hitting your skin, the warmth of the water relaxing your muscles or invigorating you. Open your mouth, let the drops hit your tongue and feel the water running over your lips and chin.

- There are a whole host of physical and mental health problems linked to smoking – but you know that already.
- Quitting suddenly, rather than gradually, increases the risk of withdrawal symptoms.

2

What is mindfulness?

Mindfulness is about:

- being alert and aware
- of what is happening within you and around you
- in this moment.[1]

It looks at paying attention to the present moment, to what is happening within you – such as your thoughts, emotions and sensations – and the world around you, without criticism or judgement. Attention and focus are needed to become more aware of what is occurring, which can in turn lead to balanced decision-making and to less rash reactions to situations. It is a way to improve your control, self-management skills and reactions to impulses. This can be useful for smokers as, over time, smoking becomes a habitual, impulsive process. Often, once it has become a habit, the thinking time between the craving for a cigarette and smoking one is very short and you don't give it much thought. Mindfulness can help you understand when you crave, what the cravings mean and why you've become psychologically addicted. More importantly, it gives you a means of dealing with the cravings and addiction, now and for the long term.

A brief history of mindfulness

Mindfulness is a component of contemplative philosophies, in this case with Buddhist roots going back 2,500 years.[2] Vital elements within Buddhist practices are meditations centring on breathing, and focusing techniques training you to be in the present moment. These practices reached Western societies, and in 1979, University of Massachusetts colleagues devised a programme based on them for people with health conditions. Mindfulness-Based Stress Reduction (MBSR) was the name given to this programme.[3]

Meditation for sceptics

The term 'meditation' can raise suspicions about its credibility, the general view being that it sends you into a trance-like state. In the context of mindfulness, this is the opposite where, rather than shutting off, it sharpens your awareness of the here and now. This allows an open attitude to dealing with present thoughts in a more receptive, non-reactive way.

In order for you to get an idea of what is currently going on inside your mind, here is an introductory practice to get you started on mindfulness.

Mindfulness practice: A Moment of Stillness

Sit in stillness for two minutes, while paying attention to what is going through your mind.

- Were there any sensations? Did anything come into your mind? If so, were they good or difficult thoughts? Did thoughts of smoking come up?
- Did you feel calmer – or more stressed? Why do you think that was? Note down as many thoughts and sensations as you can remember. When we take the time to sit in stillness, often our minds can be overrun by all the things queuing for our attention.

In the following chapters, the mindfulness practices can help you develop your focused attention, allowing you to take a step back from these thoughts and feelings.

Mindfulness gives you a chance to step back from your emotions, thoughts and reactions and allows you to see them with greater clarity.

Mindfulness is about switching on, not switching off. It's not relaxation or there to tune you out but rather to help you to focus, be present and alert and to bring your attention into this moment, right here, right now.

- It can be hard to maintain a balance as life is often busy.
- Mindfulness can be useful as a way of finding and keeping your sense of stability.

3

Life's complexities

Maintaining a balanced life can be a challenge, and a demanding schedule may leave you feeling stressed, exhausted or both. A consequence of this can be thoughts or feelings of anxiety, of depression, a decrease in self-esteem or a general level of distress and exhaustion that can come about gradually over time. This book will encourage you to look at your present circumstances and assist you in recognizing which experiences in your life, both present and past, have led you to think, feel and act as you currently do. Most importantly, it will help you create a sound sense of simply being present in your own life and the opportunity for you to make good decisions for yourself from one moment to the next. If you fully commit to mindfulness, you will in time be able to stop smoking altogether.

An advantage of mindfulness is that it can be used as a valuable and practical approach to appreciate better the *good* aspects of your life too, which can sometimes be taken for granted.

Below is a practice that can help sharpen your awareness of the present.

Mindfulness practice: Let's Go for a Walk

Focusing your attention on a seemingly simple function can ground you. This walking practice can help to settle you when you are stressed or need to rebalance your focus. You can also use it when you feel your frustrations growing.

- Take a walk wherever is convenient. Keeping your eyes half closed, bring your attention to the sensations of walking. Feel the changes in pressure as you place your feet on the ground, the rhythm of your footsteps and the movement of your arms. Slow it down and breathe in as you gently place one foot on the ground and breathe out as you place the other foot on the ground.

- Acknowledge any thoughts that come to mind and then let go of them, letting them drift away from your attention. Take a mental step back from the activities surrounding you and continue to focus on your breathing as a space forms between you and the outside world while you continue walking in a focused way.

- After a time, stand still and appreciate this moment, knowing you can take this sense of calm and clarity with you when you step back into your everyday activities.

- Mindfulness is the practice of paying attention in the present moment.
- It helps us manage the difficult times and appreciate the good ones.

4

The evidence

In recent years, the number of studies investigating the effects of mindfulness has risen sharply. Addiction, and more specifically smoking, is one of the issues starting to receive more attention.

Mindfulness for smokers: the research

- An analysis of 13 studies on mindfulness and smoking reported promising results, especially for smoking cessation, relapse prevention, number of cigarettes smoked, mindfulness helping with moderating cravings and smoking, and the development of coping strategies to deal with triggers to smoke.[1]
- Smokers who attended mindfulness meditation sessions reduced the number of cigarettes they smoked.[2]
- Smokers who received mindfulness psycho-education focusing on the idea of accepting cravings as part of the quitting process reported lower morning and evening cravings than smokers who received no mindfulness psycho-education.[3]
- Eight sessions of mindfulness training for people who smoked an average of 20 cigarettes a day led to greater reductions in cigarette use than a standard smoking cessation treatment.[4]
- The self-awareness, skills and insight learnt through mindfulness practice can positively influence the psychological, physiological and behavioural processes associated with addiction and relapse.[5]

- Mindfulness-based relapse prevention brought significant decreases in cravings.[6]
- Mindfulness can help with preventing relapses in addiction.[7]
- Mindfulness training for Smokers (MTS) taught in six weekly classes to young adults with episodes of binge drinking also found it beneficial for smoking cessation as well as treating alcohol abuse.[8]
- A mindfulness-based smoking cessation programme enabled a person with an intellectual disability who had smoked for nearly 20 years to quit smoking entirely.[9]
- Acceptance and mindfulness-based approaches are a useful treatment for individuals with co-occurring nicotine dependence and mental health disorders.[10]
- Mindfulness is an effective intervention for smokers who also have weight concerns.[11]
- Mindfulness-based relapse prevention has been found to reduce depression-related substance abuse.[12]

It is a strength not a weakness to recognize that you can benefit from support when trying to stop smoking.

Evidence for other positive impacts of mindfulness

Mindfulness has been found to have a positive effect on a number of health issues, not only smoking. Below is a list of some of these. Smoking is an addiction that can impact on a range of areas of your life. It could be that some of these issues are related to your smoking habit.

Medical conditions
- Mindfulness assists people with managing pain.[13]
- Mindfulness reduces blood pressure levels and chronic migraines.[14]
- Mindfulness improves the functioning of the immune system.[15]
- Mindfulness helps people to manage their food intake.[16]
- Mindfulness lowers the occurrence of sleep disturbances.[17]

- Mindfulness assists with multiple sclerosis, arthritis, premenstrual syndrome and Type 2 diabetes.[18]
- Mindfulness improves cancer patients' quality of life and sleep quality.[19]

Mental health

- Mindfulness lowers levels of depression and frustration.[20]
- Mindfulness reduces levels of rumination.[21]
- Mindfulness improves mood and helps maintain a balanced mood.[22]
- Mindfulness reduces the release of the stress hormone, cortisol.[23]
- Mindfulness develops the ability to feel compassion.[24]
- Mindfulness lowers levels of anxiety, pain and depression in older adults.[25]

Brain functioning

- Mindfulness training decreases frequency of mind wandering and improves memory.[26]
- Mindfulness increases grey-matter density in areas of the brain associated with learning, memory and emotional regulation.[27]

Relationships

- Secure attachments in relationships are more likely the more mindful people become.[28]
- Mindfulness increases levels of couples' satisfaction in their relationships[29] and assists in dealing with sexual dysfunction.[30]
- Mindfulness brings about less reactivity in relationships and a greater understanding and acceptance of unity, separation, intimacy and independence.[31]

General

A group of healthy people lowered their levels of stress and anxiety and increased their levels of empathy, spirituality and self-compassion through a mindfulness programme.[32]

Putting research into practice

Due to the nature of addiction, craving comes in waves. When a craving builds, you start to feel irritated, anxious or restless. It can even disrupt your ability to think clearly, to return to sleep if you awake or to finish your meal. Your mind may focus on very little other than the thought of 'I need a cigarette.' Below is a practice that will give you a moment to gather your thoughts and will steady you to the point that the urge to smoke will not be as strong as it was beforehand. It will distract you from the overriding thoughts of wanting to smoke and create a distance between you and the craving. If you focus on each moment of the task, you'll be less able to focus on your craving.

In general, it is a particularly useful practice that you can draw on whenever needed and for any reason.

Mindfulness practice: A Moment of Calm in Less than Two Minutes

This practice is an excellent introduction to how quickly and effectively focusing on your breathing can calm you. It can be done at any time or in any place when you feel stressed or are craving.

- Sit in a chair with your eyes open or closed and place one hand on your stomach, feeling the rise and fall of it (see Figure 1, opposite). Without forcing your breath in any way, silently count 'In, two, three, four' on the inbreath and 'Out, two, three, four' on the outbreath. Repeat this three times.

- Breathe in for the same amount of time as above, but count only 'In, two, three' on the inbreath and 'Out, two, three' on the outbreath. Repeat three times, then reduce it to 'In, two, Out, two' and repeat three times. Now take one breath in and one breath out, without counting. If this feels difficult, think 'In' and 'Out' to the rhythm of your breathing. Repeat three times.

- Take a moment to feel the effect this practice has had on you. Do you feel less tense? Has your craving subsided? Know that returning to a more balanced state of mind can be as simple as breathing.

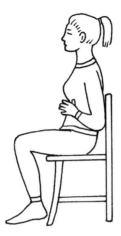

Figure 1   Sitting in a chair with one hand resting on the stomach

- Evidence shows that mindfulness is useful for stopping smoking and assisting in the treatment of other physical and mental health issues.
- Many studies have found mindfulness to be an effective approach in bettering one's life and improving the quality of it.

Part 2

The smoking habit

5

The stress response

What is the stress response?

We all feel stress at times, even on a daily basis, and it can be a difficult and exhausting experience. Smokers often have a cigarette when they feel stressed as a way of getting away from the stressful situation or as time out. What is often forgotten is that the body and mind function together as one system; they do not work separately from each other. Consequently, when we are psychologically or physically stressed our bodies react.

Mindfulness can help you become more aware of what makes you feel stressed as well as when and why you get stressed. More importantly, it can help reduce the physical impact stress has on your body. Figure 2 (overleaf) shows a very basic example of a link between stress and smoking.

Stress levels can grow steadily without your being fully conscious of them. Your body is constantly reacting to your thoughts and emotions, including stress, as stress begins in your mind, which then triggers a chain reaction in your body.

As a result of evolution, the stress response is an inherent part of our survival mechanism. If danger was anticipated (such as a tiger suddenly appearing), the stress response provided a warning signal and prepared our body to fight or flee the present threat, and this warning system was frequently the difference between life and death. However, in the present day, when the stress mechanism is activated

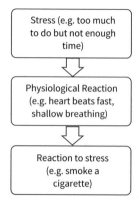

Figure 2 **Stress flow chart**

more frequently by demands and pressures than hungry tigers, your mind doesn't realize that you aren't in true physical danger. This occurs because your mind cannot distinguish between a real threat and a perceived one, so that, for example, your body responds in the same way to seeing a tiger jump out at you as it does to getting agitated in traffic or being stressed by your workload. Your brain doesn't know that the pressure you feel under at work, a perceived threat,

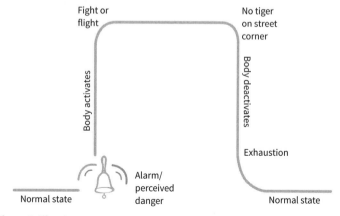

Figure 3 **The stress response**

isn't a warning that you are in true physical danger as you would be if a tiger popped its head around the corner (see Figure 3).

A physiological reaction to stress occurs via the sympathetic nervous system, which switches you into 'go' mode. Once the situation of threat has passed, your body should return to its normal state. The method of the body returning to its normal state is via the parasympathetic system, which puts you back into 'rest' mode (see Table 2).

Table 2 Sympathetic and parasympathetic systems

Sympathetic system	Parasympathetic system
• Adrenalin and cortisol release into blood • Breathing rate increases • Heart rate levels rise • Energy directed to heart, muscles and breathing • Digestive process shuts down	• Noradrenalin released into blood • Breathing rate decreases • Heart rate levels lower • Energy redirected to other organs in body that help with digestion, absorption, excretion and other essential functions

However, when stress is continually experienced, your sympathetic nervous system remains in a more active state than it needs to be

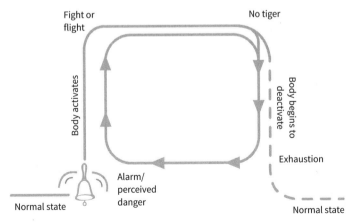

Figure 4 The chronic/ongoing stress response

(see Figure 4). This phenomenon is extremely important because, over time, this can bring about both physical and psychological problems due to your mind and body becoming exhausted.

What non-stop stress can cause

There is known to be a link between stress and multiple conditions, such as:

- damage to organ and memory cells
- fatty deposits around waist
- increased aging
- hypertension
- heart disease
- diabetes
- pain conditions
- infertility
- loss of libido
- decreased work performance
- distorted thinking
- irritable bowel syndrome
- depression
- anxiety/panic attacks
- rheumatoid arthritis
- cancer
- sleep difficulties
- impotence
- relationship difficulties
- decrease in quality of life.

People smoke for many reasons, such as the enjoyment and satisfaction of it or as an attempt to manage stress, difficult emotions – such as fear, anger, frustration – or even boredom. It is also associated with being sociable – as when huddled outside a building or in the garden with other smokers – and sometimes smoking is a way of having a few minutes of quiet on one's own. However, the calming effects of a cigarette wear off quickly and stress levels will return to their previous state. Research has shown that although smoking provides immediate stress relief, it increases stress levels long term.[1]

Doing the mindfulness practices in this book on a regular basis can assist you in becoming more aware of when you're stressed, under pressure or when you're doing something associated with pleasure, and in managing your response to it in a healthier way. With practice it could mean that the next time this situation comes about you can step back for a moment and acknowledge: 'I'm stressing about this' or 'I don't have to stand outside and smoke after a meal'. Taking a moment to evaluate during such times is far more helpful than one realizes. It can be an opportunity for you to recognize the various options you have to respond to the situation and what you're presently feeling, rather than being limited to just the one option of smoking a cigarette. This may sound obvious but we frequently get so entrenched in our ways that we come to believe that other options aren't really possible or worth trying. We also have a strong tendency to revert to what's familiar, even when we know it isn't the most useful or helpful option.

Mindfulness practices should be done when you're stressed *and* when you're not. The practice below is to help you become more aware of one of your senses; that is, how you respond to an everyday taste. Much like smoking, meal times can seem so normal that the process becomes largely unconscious. You may eat without fully appreciating the tastes, textures, smells and sensations that can come with it.

Mindfulness practice: Mindful Eating

This practice can bring a sense of quietness to meal times and allow people to enjoy their food more fully. Smoking withdrawal symptoms can include strong hunger cravings, so this would be an ideal time to do the practice.

- Take a piece of fruit, chocolate or any food that's not too hard to chew. Eat it as normal.

- Take another piece and place it on your tongue. Without chewing, focus on the sensation. What does it feel like? Can you taste anything you previously hadn't noticed?

- Chew slowly. Does it make a sound? Is it difficult to resist the urge to swallow the food?

- The stress response is an innate survival mechanism but it can have a number of negative effects on our physical and mental health when it is continually experienced.

- Stress levels can decrease through mindfulness as the practices not only bring down your physiological response to stress but also give you the internal headspace to recognize and consider that there are different options open to you as a way of dealing with your stress, distress, boredom or daily pleasures.

6

The addiction

The addiction cycle

An addiction is complex and often works in a cyclical manner. An outline of this is summarized in Figure 5 (overleaf). Put simply, it goes in the cycle of trigger, craving, habit, use, comedown and repeat.

In general terms, a **trigger** can be physiological but usually stems from an emotion – for example, feeling stressed or upset about something. Having a meal or a drink can also be triggers. The trigger sends a signal to the brain that leads to a **craving**. The craving is your body wanting nicotine. However, there is also a psychological craving, which is more to do with the triggers and the associations you have with smoking. A craving will persistently push you to smoke and can be likened to someone poking you again and again on the arm until you react.

Making the craving more difficult to ignore is the **habit** aspect of the cycle. The habit comes about from smoking over a period of time. Your body knows that you've previously been comforted by, or found pleasure in, smoking, so there is a learnt association that you can be comforted or pleased by it again. These tempting feelings of satisfaction and familiarity result in the **use** of a cigarette. This will bring feelings of pleasure and possibly relief. The final stage is the **comedown**. After the short-term nicotine effects end, the 'high' will wear off and you will revert to your normal state. You may feel deflated, defeated or guilty that you have smoked at this stage, if you're trying

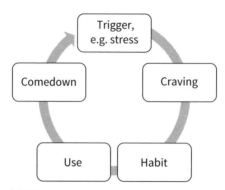

Figure 5 The addiction cycle

to quit. If not, then you may continue with whatever you were doing until the next trigger or craving.

The good news is that mindfulness can help at every stage of this cycle, until the cycle becomes weaker and the connections that hold it together are gradually lessened or even broken down. Ideally you should be aiming to use mindfulness at the trigger stage, preventing the rest of the cycle occurring. Mindfulness can help you become more aware of your specific triggers, such as the situations in which you're most likely to smoke. This may be at the pub, on your lunch break or when you see someone else smoking, for example. Alternatively it may be specific feelings, such as feeling bored, stressed or relaxed. Triggers will never be completely got rid of, but becoming more aware of them is a crucial first step that makes the craving and habit stages less difficult to manage.

Using mindfulness practices at the trigger stage won't initially stop the subsequent stages of the addiction cycle happening as they're well ingrained and it takes time to shift familiar responses. Fortunately the practices can still be used at the later stages too. At the craving stage, you may feel restless or anxious and perhaps have a feeling of being 'on edge'. There are numerous mindfulness practices that can be used to settle your thoughts and calm your emotions, such as placing your hand on your abdomen and breathing into it (see the practice 'A Moment of Calm in Less than Two Minutes' in Chapter 4) or taking a short mindful walk (see the practice 'Let's Go for a Walk' in Chapter 3). Experiment and find what works best for you. 'The Mountain Meditation', a practice to be found in Chapter 9, can be particularly useful in reinforcing your stability and balance and starting to shift any thoughts of being helpless over your addiction.

Furthermore, even at the comedown stage, mindfulness can support you to accept what has just happened and remind you that the past is the past and the present moment offers a new beginning. It can all feel a bit gloomy after the nicotine wears off. However, mindfulness is about developing feelings of self-compassion. It can help you to stay away from harsh self-criticism and remind you that your next craving offers another chance to make a healthier choice for yourself.

This isn't about making excuses for having a cigarette but more about recognizing that harsh judgement won't help you and that each experience offers you another opportunity to do something different. If a toddler is learning to walk and continually falls, you wouldn't jump in with criticism and reprimands. Instead, you would be understanding and encourage the child to keep trying, as it will eventually happen. The same goes for you with the falls and steps forward of stopping smoking.

Additional aids

There are numerous additional aids that can be used alongside mindfulness to increase your chances of quitting smoking successfully, if you feel you need them. Some of these you will probably have heard of or tried, perhaps more than once. If they helped in some way in the past then you may wish to try them again, but in combination with the practices and ideas in this book.

If you wish to find out more about these quitting aids, please consult your doctor or pharmacist. Some of these aids are:

- nicotine replacement therapy (NRT): skin patches, chewing gum, mouth spray, nasal spray, inhalators, tablets and lozenges
- stop-smoking medication: Zyban (bupropion), Champix (varenicline)
- electronic cigarettes or e-cigarettes.

Smoking can interfere with some medications, so when smoking you need a higher dose of those specific ones. This also means that if you stop smoking you may then need a lower dose. However, it is essential to speak to your doctor or health professional before adjusting your own medications.

Medications that are affected by smoking are:

- antidepressants, such as amitriptyline and mirtazapine
- antipsychotics, especially clozapine, olanzapine and haloperidol
- benzodiazepines, such as diazepam
- opiates, such as methadone.[1]

It's worth recognizing that it's easy to use an aid such as an e-cigarette or gum as a substitute, but that substitutes can, in turn, become a form of addiction. E-cigarettes especially, and the trend in vaping, maintain the addictive behaviours and rituals associated with smoking, so that you aren't really having to address and shift the very things that keep you addicted or open to relapse. E-cigarettes still contain nicotine and other harmful chemicals and they aren't yet widely regulated, so one can't be sure what each brand contains. In addition, little is known about the health risks associated with e-cigarettes.[2]

It should be noted, however, that if you choose to use any of these aids, it does not mean you should stop using mindfulness. They should be used alongside mindfulness, not instead of it. Although the additional aids can be of significant use in terms of providing you with smaller, steadier levels of nicotine to reduce your reliance on the stimulant gradually, they will not be effective in helping you deal with the psychology of the habit and the ingrained behaviours. It is only by addressing these issues that you'll be able to stop smoking now and forever.

This is where mindfulness is essential, as re-evaluating and adjusting your attitude and approach towards smoking is arguably the most important step to quitting. With mindfulness you will also be able to ride the waves of your craving and respond to them in a more aware and controlled way.

The phrase 'Surf the urge' is often used in addiction work. Urges or cravings are like waves, some small and rippling, others frighteningly powerful and all-consuming. You need to learn to surf – and mindfulness is your surfboard.

The next practice focuses your awareness and attention on your body, encouraging you to engage with each area. You may initially find it unusual as it's about breathing into the different parts of your body. It's worth trying as most people really enjoy it and find it useful, especially men for some reason.

Mindfulness practice: Body Focus

The Body Focus practice helps you become more in tune with your body and may help you be more aware of the parts that are in particular affected by cigarette cravings. You may then be able to relax certain areas actively, when they feel tense.

- Find a quiet place and choose a position that works well for you. Ideally, lie flat on your back on a blanket, carpet or bed, with a cushion for your head if this feels better (Figure 6). Place your legs on a chair, straight or bent if it's more comfortable, when on the floor (Figure 7, overleaf). If lying down is difficult for you, sit in a chair that provides sufficient support

Figure 6 Lying on the floor

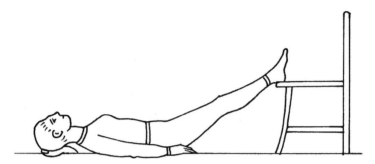

Figure 7 Lying on the floor with feet up on a chair

(Figure 8, opposite). If sitting is not ideal, you can stand steadily against a wall (Figure 9, opposite).

- When the audio download says 'Breathe into your toes' or any other part of your body, it is meant metaphorically. Physically we can only breathe into our lungs, so it's about imagining the breath moving through your body, bringing attention to it and relaxing that area.
- Most people fall asleep when first doing this practice. If you do so on the second attempt, sit upright until you're able to do it without drifting off to sleep.
- With this practice and any of the following ones, if you start to feel drowsy, shift your position and bring your attention and focus back to the instructions of the guided meditation that you are listening to.

The following is a transcript of part of the practice to give you an idea of what it's about; see also Figures 6–9 for the different positions you can use.

🔊 Listen to the Body Focus practice from the audio download of guided meditations. After the practice, take a few moments to think about your response to it. Did you give yourself the time and space to do the practice?

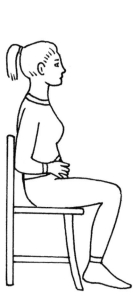

Figure 8 Sitting in a chair

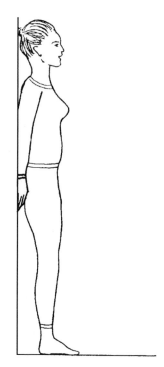

Figure 9 Standing against a wall

Extract from the transcript of the Body Focus practice

The intention is to bring awareness to the different parts of the body without moving or stretching them in any way. It is about experiencing the sensations within your body, making no demands on it.

As you breathe in and out, become aware that this is your body, all of it, for whatever it is: the parts that work well and keep you alive, and the parts that are damaged and in pain.

Now focus on the big toe of your left foot. Become aware of the existence of this part of your body and the sensations that might be there. Let your attention go deep into the toe, not moving it, just observing it and feeling whatever is or isn't happening in it at this moment. If you feel no sensations, that too is fine. Simply acknowledge whatever is there.

Now move your focus to the little toe on the left foot – and to all the toes. Become aware of the feelings within the toes, acknowledge them, and breathe deep into the toes on an inbreath. And on an outbreath let go of your awareness of the toes, letting their existence drift and dissolve from your mind.

Now bring your attention to the sole of your left foot, focusing on any sensations deep within the foot, aware of the air against it, your instep, the heel against the floor. Breathe in and out of it, and on the outbreath let go of your awareness of it and bring it to the top of the left foot, becoming familiar with the sensations in this part of your body, of all the small bones that make up the foot. Breathing all the way into it, and then on an outbreath, let it dissolve from awareness.

Move your focus to the left ankle, feeling and acknowledging whatever it is that is there, aware of the bones that come together to form a joint. Breathing into it and out of it, let it go. Now focus on the foot and ankle as a whole, breathing deep into it. Let your breath travel, in your mind's eye, all the way down from the nostrils, through the chest and abdomen, down the left leg and into the foot and ankle, aware of the oxygen coming to it – and when it gets there, release it and let the breath travel all the way back out through the nostrils, and on an outbreath, let the foot and ankle dissolve from your awareness.

Remember, the practices are there to help you to switch on, not to switch off.

- Addiction is a cycle; mindfulness can be used to target each stage of the cycle and weaken its hold over you.
- There are smoking aids available that can be used alongside mindfulness, not instead of it. The aids do not adjust what is behind the behaviour, whereas mindfulness does.

7

The bigger picture

What influences your well-being?

A model that illustrates which factors come together to influence your well-being is the biopsychosocial model, which draws attention to three different factor groups: biological, psychological and social. Figure 10 illustrates the biopsychosocial model.

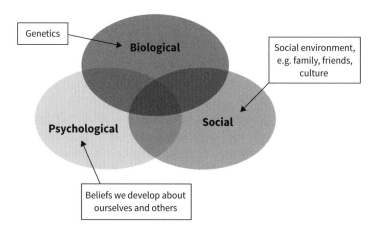

Figure 10 The biopsychosocial model

What is the use of the biopsychosocial model?

The biopsychosocial model can assist your understanding of the interactions between your mind and body and how they impact on each other. All three factor groups – biological, psychological and social – are vital in helping you to identify who you are in the here and now and what has led you to be how you are. Through considering these factors you can come to understand more about what led you to start smoking, why you still smoke and what it will take for you to quit successfully. Using the column headings shown in Table 3, write down what you think about yourself and where and why these beliefs may have come about.

Table 3 Biological, psychological and social influences

Biological	Psychological	Social

A great deal of your physiological and some of your psychological characteristics are inherited from your parents through genetics. In fact, research has shown how there is a genetic predisposition – that is, a possibility but not a given – as to how likely someone is to develop a smoking experience into an addiction.[1] However, your experiences growing up also greatly shape your development. For instance, if one or both of your parents smoked when you were a child, this role modelling can increase the likelihood of you also forming an addiction. Similarly, if you were part of a group of friends in your teenage years where most of you smoked, your peers may have influenced you. Like genetic factors, your social environment, such as family and peer affiliations, has been discovered to be linked to becoming a smoker.[2]

The psychodynamic approach

The psychodynamic approach is an essential part of the 'psycho' part of the biopsychosocial model. It is based on the theory that your experiences from childhood into adulthood considerably affect who you are in your adult years, and how you act. The common theory is that if you are given regular, reliable and engaged care in your early years, you will grow to believe that you are lovable and valuable. On the other hand, if the care in your early years was unpredictable or lacking in boundaries, appropriate feedback or warmth, this can negatively influence how you view yourself as an adult. Research has revealed a link between childhood stress and the formation of a smoking addiction in early adulthood.[3]

In terms of any distress you could presently be feeling in your life, it isn't necessarily true that one factor will be the precise cause of another. However, biological, psychological, social and early life experiences are unavoidably linked to one another. Becoming better aware of and alert to these factors can help you to see how you function as an individual, gain a clearer picture of what fits where, make sense of it and place it within a context.[4] Using the previous table as a foundation, consider some of the factors past and present that could have influenced your smoking habit and list them on a sheet of paper, using the column headings shown in Table 4 (overleaf).

Important

By engaging more with yourself as a whole and by understanding the events that have brought you to where you are now, feelings and memories may come to mind that could be upsetting. Should this happen, acknowledge them but manage them by listening to music or talking to a friend, for example. If the feelings are too distressing, you should speak to a qualified therapist. Therapy is simply about two people coming together to take care of your life and to help you understand what is happening. It helps to develop skills to manage aspects of your life using the strengths you already have and building other resources from which you may benefit.

Table 4 Influences on your smoking habit

Biological	Psychological	Social	Early experiences	Purpose of smoking

Meditation or sitting positions

The meditation positions, or sitting positions as they are often called, were illustrated in Figures 6–9 in Chapter 6 as examples. You may find it more comfortable sitting upright on your bed or cross-legged on the sofa. Some people find sitting on a meditation cushion very focusing. These are often large, firm, round cushions called zafus that help you to keep upright. It is important whenever you are sitting for any period of time to make sure that the level of your hips is higher than your knees, even when sitting in a chair. If you find a zafu comfortable but too low, you can put large yoga blocks underneath it (yoga blocks are firm blocks of foam that look like small slabs). This can be a very pleasant and open way to do the 5-minute and 20-minute Mindful Awareness breathing practices. There is no need for you to suffer, so use props, cushions, blankets or anything else to help you feel comfortable, but always try to keep your back upright, your chest and heart area open and your head gently balanced on your neck. There should be a softness and openness to your approach to all the practices. There will always be noise but try to find a place where you won't be interrupted, and ensure that your mobile phone is turned down. This meditation can be done whether sitting at an office desk or on a bench in the garden.

There is no perfect way

When doing these practices there is no right or wrong way, no set goal or score sheet. Inevitably your mind will drift when meditating, your thoughts will intrude and your concentration will flit about at a rapid pace. This will happen at first and even after many years. The aim is not to empty the mind but to become aware of what is happening with it; your thoughts, emotions and urges. Acknowledge whatever is there without reacting, simply saying 'Thought' when a thought comes up or 'Feeling' when a feeling emerges. It's about recognizing the activity for what it is – for example, thinking – and then letting it be there without attending to it. Whenever your mind drifts or gets into an activity, acknowledge it, step away from it and bring your attention back to your breathing – focus and refocus, no matter how often this happens. Rest assured, it will happen over and over again because that's what minds do – they think, connect, make links, activate emotions and impulses and react. Your mind is simply doing its job, and your job is to focus its energy and train it to refocus that energy either on your breathing or, at other times in your life, on a situation or experience.

The main issue is that you keep doing the practices. Each time you do you're developing the structures in your brain, your emotional resilience and your own internal sense of stability and belief.

Mindful awareness

The following practice is one that you will come to rely on for years to come. It's one of the key meditations central to mindfulness practice, and its benefits are far reaching. It truly is worth doing on a regular basis.

Mindfulness practice: Mindful Awareness

Mindful awareness is about becoming aware of what is happening within yourself, which encourages you to bring your focus and attention to your internal experiences and how they shift.

🔊 There are two options for this practice on the audio download: a 20-minute version and a 5-minute version. Begin with the 5-minute version, and once this feels familiar you can then move on to the 20-minute one if you can. Ideally, do the 20-minute version a few times a week, and the 5-minute one on the other days.

Below you will see a transcript of the 5-minute Mindful Awareness practice, which is a breathing practice. It has been included to show you that there is nothing strange or peculiar about the practices. You are breathing anyway, so these practices help you focus your breathing and use it in a remarkably helpful way.

Transcript of the Mindful Awareness practice (5-minute version)
With your eyes closed, while being alert and awake, bring your attention to your breathing and to the movement of the breath as it comes in and out of your body. Simply observe your breathing – watching the path it takes as it travels in at the nose, down to the abdomen and then out again through the nose.

Stay focused on the breath, without forcing it in any way. Be here, with each inbreath and with each outbreath, letting one follow on from the other.

Use your breath as an anchor. Allow the breath to anchor you to the centre within your abdomen, that part that is stable, focused and present. Follow the breath to your anchor, bringing with it a new beginning and with each outbreath a letting go.

Be aware of each breath nourishing and grounding you, renewing and letting go, one breath following the other. Allow it to bring with it a stillness and a feeling of balance, grounding you right here, right now. Letting it anchor you, gently and kindly, to this moment, and to this moment.

As the intensity begins to ease, let your attention spread to include all of your body, and engage your breath into a rhythmic flow that moves in and out of your body as a whole.

Gradually let your awareness begin to take in the sounds around you and within you, simply letting them exist in harmony with you, as you breathe. Sit in stillness, in this moment.

Feel grounded, feel balanced. Gently allow all of your senses to be awake, to be alert and alive to all that is happening within you and around you. Acknowledge with kindness that you spent this time living each moment of your life, with whatever came with it, in a mindful, balanced and open way, and that you now have the choice of how you wish to live this moment of your life, and this moment.

You'll notice with all the guided meditations that there is a bong sound at the beginning and end of each to help prepare you for the beginning and end of each one.

Keeping tabs

It is helpful to take a moment to think about your progress, so a week or two after regularly practising mindful awareness, give some thought to your experience with mindfulness so far. Have you noticed any effects from doing the practices? Have you been managing any situations differently?

Think about your attitude towards the practices. Have you given yourself the time to focus on them or have you put them off? Your attitude can reveal important aspects of your approach towards other areas of your life. If you've avoided the practices, then perhaps this stage will be a turning point for your motivation. With each breath is a new beginning. If you've approached the practices in a motivated manner, hold on to this motivation as it can help you to develop your own sense of resilience and belief that you can make a difference in your life.

Recognizing what's happening

As noted already, people frequently feel depressed or anxious when they stop smoking. Some of this is due to the nicotine withdrawal, but smoking can also act as a way of avoiding feelings or situations. Consequently, if you're not smoking then these feelings will come up. For example, you may have reached for a cigarette when you started to feel lonely or had one when a discussion started that made you feel agitated or become angry. People also use smoking after sex to avoid further intimacy or as an escape from the situation. You may be shy and find it easier speaking to one or two people outside rather than the crowd inside at the party. These feelings are still inside you, but now you need to work with them or do something to diffuse them – other than smoking a cigarette.

It's the same with stress. People smoke as they think it helps them to cope. It only acts as a sticking plaster, and learning to manage stress in more helpful ways will stand you in good stead in most areas of your life.

The bottom line is that if you really do want to quit, you will need to deal with, or learn to manage, the feelings and situations that were being clouded by, or avoided by, smoking. The word 'smokescreen' comes to mind as it is a very accurate concept and visual picture that describes what is being discussed here.

- Biological, psychological and social factors as well as early child-hood experiences all affect the development of your personality and your view of yourself, others and the world.
- Mindfulness can increase your awareness of what factors led to the development of your smoking habit and how you deal with the quitting process.

8

No magic remedy

Mindfulness is most definitely not a magic solution to your problems, nor will it get you to stop smoking overnight. It's good that it isn't magic, otherwise it would take away your control over your life. However, what it will do is improve your ability and resilience to surf the waves of your cravings, though you need to do the work to feel the benefits. The more you do it, the greater the benefits, and the outcomes will feel almost magical in some moments.

Connecting the pieces

Imagine a jigsaw puzzle with all the pieces scattered. Liken this jigsaw to your mind, each piece representing different emotions, sensations and thoughts. Unless you commit to the task and give yourself the time to focus on connecting the pieces, they will stay scattered and the full picture will never be seen. However, if you choose to pay attention to the task then all the pieces can, one by one, be linked, and the relevance of one piece to another can slowly be uncovered. Mindfulness enables you to recognize and acknowledge the pieces of your mind that were previously scattered and then to connect or reconnect them. This makes it easier for you to step back and see the bigger picture for what it really is.

Now is only the start of what will be a long but rewarding road to stopping smoking. The process of you smoking has become, with time and repetition, a familiar reaction, a habit. It is important, in fact essential, that you raise the reactive, habitual response of smoking into consciousness in order to tackle it in a systematic and thought-through way. Being mindful helps you to highlight your habit and makes it clear to see.

No judgement or criticism is required, only the act of awareness and acknowledgment and the realization that each moment brings with it the possibility of a new beginning. The Buddhists refer to 'beginner's mind', which translates into our bringing into each situation, no matter how familiar or repetitive, a fresh attitude as though that situation is happening for the first time. It is remarkable how this approach can shift old and entrenched perspectives.

- Mindfulness is not a magic solution that will instantly fix all your problems.
- The more committed you are to practising mindfulness, the more likely you are to feel the benefits in your attitude, health and quality of life.

Part 3

How can I make the changes I want?

9

Living in the now

When you light a cigarette as you have done tens, hundreds or thousands of times before, you are making the decision to light it based on a background of familiarity, repetition and reward, which have all come together to form the habit you have today. At times, it may be that you have no real urge to smoke but the habit is so ingrained in your daily life that you will do so anyway.

When caught in a cycle of addiction it can feel extremely difficult to break it. However, mindfulness can help bring greater attention and focus to your present decisions and provide more thinking space for you to consider the alternatives to smoking every time you go to light a cigarette. This won't stop you smoking right away. Nevertheless you won't be puffing away as you may have done before. With mindfulness practice and experience comes clearer, more reflective and more conscious thought and decision-making.

Make your brain a better brain: the more you do the practices, the greater the effect they have on the structure of your brain.

I-QUIT

You always have the choice as to whether or not you smoke as it isn't something you're forced to do. Despite this it can feel as though you have no choice at times, as levels of control are weakened by relentless cravings and cycles of habit, as well as the anticipated enjoyment or outcome.

Fighting cravings is difficult, frustrating and exhausting. The following step-by-step approach, '**I-QUIT**', may help you deal with the waves of craving:

I – IDENTIFY the craving for what it is when it first occurs. Observe how it makes you feel physically and psychologically. Does it make your heart race or your hands clammy? Are you feeling agitated? Is it actually a craving for a cigarette or for something else, such as liquid, food or sex?

Q – QUIET the mind. Once you have identified the different elements of the craving, try to slow everything down.

U – UNLATCH yourself from the craving by stepping back from it and creating a space between yourself and it. Don't do battle with the craving, step away from it.

I – INHALE. Take a few measured and focused breaths and with each inbreath draw in a sense of calm and control and with each outbreath imagine you are breathing out the power of the craving from your body.

T – TAKE CONTROL. Detach yourself from the battle with your craving and breathe deep into your anchor, into that part of you that is stable, anchored and balanced. Accept the moment of craving that has gripped you and remind yourself that although it is there you don't have to give in to it. Try not to get frustrated that it is present, simply acknowledge it and ride the wave of it. You have your surfboard so now is the time to use it.

Always remember that no matter how strong the desire or the feeling that has descended upon you, it has in fact come from within you. It's generated from inside of you, by you, which means you can now take control of it – not always control it, but take control *of* it. The difference between the two is that you may not be able to lessen the intensity of it or when it happens but you can – yes, you can – control how you respond to it.

Think about other options and how else you could respond to this craving. You can distract yourself by jumping up and down, dancing about, singing, shouting, talking to a friend on the phone, going for a quick walk, drinking a glass of water – anything that refocuses your attention. This is so important when you're craving because you need to shift the energy of the craving on to something different. It's the same energy but that focus and drive must be distracted and refocused away from the craving and on to something else.

The actual craving only lasts a few moments, so each time you redirect that energy you're giving yourself another chance of not smoking. If you do light up a cigarette or take a puff, don't waste time feeling angry or ashamed afterwards. It's happened. Think about why you did it, as this type of reflection can give you awareness of how you approach things. It can also give you a sense of control over the next response you have to a craving.

This progression of steps will better equip you to ride out the cravings rather than impulsively act on them without much thought.

What to do if you have a cigarette

- Accept that it's a slip, not a tragedy.
- Acknowledge the relapse.
- Don't do the all-or-nothing routine – just get back on track as soon as you can.
- Recognize the trigger.
- Make a mental note of how you can avoid that trigger or triggers next time.
- There's no point feeling ashamed – use that energy to get back to quitting.
- Ask for help, support and aids, such as NRT or medication (see Chapter 6).
- Use the help.

Be on guard and know that you are vulnerable and that quitting is a struggle – so avoid trigger situations and don't be tempted to take even a puff of a cigarette. Your physical brain is waiting and urging you to relapse and your psychological mind is playing tricks with you, telling you you'll feel so much better if you have just one cigarette and that you're strong enough to stop at one. You aren't – this is an addiction. What you do have is the ability to stand steadfast and take control. Find ideas that help you out, like keeping busy, distracting yourself rather than dwelling on the craving. If you're at a party, go and help in the kitchen or with the cooking rather than stand outside bemoaning your fate that you can't smoke. You really need to step up to yourself if you want to succeed.

This is pointless

It's easy to dismiss things at this point as being useless or silly. Now is the very time that you must suspend judgement and find a way around your scepticism and the barrier to stopping. You won't know what works until you try different things.

Similar to **I-QUIT**, the mindfulness practice below, called the Mountain Meditation, can help you to stand strong during a craving.

Mindfulness practice: The Mountain Meditation

The Mountain Meditation is designed to create a sense of stability, balance and well-being. It is about claiming this moment and this space for yourself and anchoring yourself, no matter how distressing life may be. It is a reminder of your personal resilience, reassuring you that you can weather any storm, even in the face of craving.

🔊 Listen to the Mountain Meditation audio download. Once you've listened to that, think about how you face difficulties, the storms you've weathered and the times you thought you couldn't cope or that life wasn't going to get better. Hold in your mind what you think helped you get through it.

Below is a transcript of the Mountain Meditation, which you can find on the audio download.

Transcript of the Mountain Meditation

Stand with your feet hip-width apart so that you can balance yourself. Keep your knees soft and your hips loose, imagining there is a small weight attached to your tailbone (coccyx). Tuck your navel in towards your spine as though you are pulling in your stomach to tighten your belt. Relax your shoulders into your back, lightly tuck in your chin, and let your head balance on top of your spine. Breathe in, and on an outbreath let unwanted tension be released. On an inbreath take in a feeling of relaxed strength.

As you stand, be aware of your breath moving in at the nostrils, down the back of the throat, into the chest and down into the abdomen, and then its movement from the abdomen, through the chest and throat and out through the nose. Allow a natural rhythm of breathing; not forcing the breath in or out in any way.

While standing here, feel the weight of your body in your feet, firm against the earth, and that the earth can carry your weight with confidence. Let your breath feel as if it is moving all the way down into your feet, giving them strength and stability. Now let the breath move into your ankles, strengthening them, and now into the calves. Let it flow into your knees, without locking them, and then into your thighs. Move the breath and steadiness into your hips, genitals, buttocks and abdomen, and let this area of your body feel strong but relaxed.

Allow the breath and strength to move up your spine at the back, through your stomach and chest, eventually reaching your shoulders, checking that they are relaxed. Your arms are becoming stronger and part of the mountain, stabilizing you, balancing you. Let it move into your neck and jaw, into the skull, ears, face, eyes and right up to the top of your head.

Now, in your mind's eye, move the breath to the base of your spine and thread it like a piece of string through each vertebra, from the tailbone, up through the pelvis, the lower back, the middle of your back, the shoulder-blade area, the back of the neck and all the way to the top of your head, where it exits and is held gently but firmly on a hook, allowing your body to hold itself.

Feel the sensation of this, of your body standing like a mountain, fixed and firm, gracious and solid. The mountain is stable and grand – the earth beneath it, the sky and air around it. The weather changes, the seasons move from one to another but the mountain remains. Feel the strength of the earth beneath you, solid and powerful, and your body open and alert, as you stand grounded and dignified in this space.

No matter how chaotic life may seem at times, you already have coping skills that you use on a daily basis and in more stressful situations. Now you can build and develop even more resilience. Find that one thing within yourself, no matter how small, that you know is strong and firm, and remind yourself of it each day.

Thoughts, emotions and experiences are transient, but the core of you is constant and enduring. By engaging in practices such as the Mountain Meditation, you are reinforcing your capacity to choose wellness over distress. Mindfulness is as much about celebrating your achievements, success and health as it is about negotiating the more difficult or negative experiences of your life.

Centring on the present moment can increase your understanding of what has happened in the past and better your chances of a calmer, more grounded future.

Remember to use **I-QUIT** whenever you crave.

- Each new craving offers a chance to take a step towards quitting.
- Identify the physical and psychological elements of the craving, accept the craving for what it is and look at how you can respond to it in a way that will help you make the choice that's right for your intention of not smoking.

10

Stop and be mindful

One of the aims of practising mindfulness, within this context, is to bring to the forefront of your mind that smoking is not your only option to deal with life's problems or desires as there are other healthier choices available to you. You already know that, but you may have struggled in the past to find something that worked longer term. Mindfulness practices help expand your ability to reflect on your thoughts and emotions and act upon them as you wish to, rather than react to them automatically.

STOP and be mindful.

Deciding to avoid or run away from the emotions and thoughts that distress you has the potential to make them more extreme in the long term.[1] Although your thoughts are part of who you are, they don't actually exist outside of your mind. Ultimately, thoughts are temporary and transient; they come and go and don't remain forever. They can return repeatedly but each time they will drift off. You can learn to choose how you wish to act on them through paying attention to your responses and opening yourself to other options.

When you stop and consider before you act, you become the leader of your life.

Picture a stressful situation. For example, you may be tired from work and short tempered as a result. How will you react to these emotions? Imagine it to be a multiple-choice exam question with several answers. It's only by stopping and thinking about each one that you give yourself a chance to make the best choice you can. Creating a chart, using the column headings shown in Table 5, will allow you to keep track of how mindfulness is helping you learn a more considered or thought-through approach to decision-making.

Table 5 Keeping track

Situations where I tend to react negatively, impulsively or in a way that is unhelpful to me	How I now respond to each or some of these situations using mindfulness	How I could respond in the future if I didn't use mindfulness this time

---

Mindfulness practice: Choosing to Refocus

- If you notice a temptation to smoke, take a few mindful breaths, anchoring yourself to the present and to that stable part of yourself while you observe your thoughts and impulses. Recognize that it is just that, a thought or impulse, and that you need not attach any significance to it or react to it.

- Just because it's difficult to say 'No' doesn't mean you shouldn't.

- Sit quietly with any emotions associated with the thought or craving, then start to shift your attention on to an aspect of your present experience that feels kinder; perhaps the warmth of the sunshine or the soft rug under your feet. You can jump up and down, dance or sing (as mentioned in the previous chapter), if that's what shifts the energy and focus, and then sit quietly. No matter how small the sensation, appreciate it.

- Choosing to focus and refocus your attention is one way mindfulness practices help to develop emotional resilience as well as alter the structure of your brain.

- Never underestimate the power of focusing on this moment.

Keep in mind that you can crave without actually smoking. This works in two ways, the one being that you can crave a cigarette but decide not to have one, and the other that you can crave even when you've stopped smoking.

- Smoking is not your only option as a reaction to stress, anxiety or a need for satisfaction or pleasure.
- Mindfulness can help you consider your decisions before making them, thereby stepping in to prevent them from being automatic or reckless choices.

11

Caring for yourself

It is so easy to be critical of yourself and focus on your bad points. It's likely that you, just like so many others, don't allow yourself to stop and feel kindness towards yourself or to recognize all the good that you do.[1] It's a difficult skill to learn at first and can feel strange and uncomfortable. However, self-care mindfulness practices can help you develop compassion towards yourself rather than berating yourself all the time. In the more difficult moments, it can be a way of helping you to be less harsh, softer and kinder towards yourself, which in turn can lessen stress and reduce the urge to smoke. Below is an example of a self-care meditation. It's worth doing as you'll be surprised how personal and intimate it can feel.

Mindfulness practice: Self-care Meditation

This meditation is a starting point for developing a kind and caring attitude towards yourself. Sit quietly in any comfortable position and take a few breaths to settle yourself.

Repeat the following phrases to yourself:

- May I be happy and healthy.
- May I accept myself for all that I am.
- May I live my life with ease.

Repeat these phrases a number of times, even when it feels difficult, as we sometimes doubt that we are worthy and deserving of happiness. You can change the wording to suit your own ideas of generosity, kindness and care towards yourself.

A wandering mind

It's important to repeat what was previously said about this as once you take it on board it will certainly help keep you on track: you may have difficulty holding your attention and your mind will drift here, there and everywhere. This is normal, as minds are meant to drift and heads have thoughts inside them, so there's no need to give up when this happens or to get frustrated. Simply bring your attention back to your breathing, back to the practice. Each time you do that your ability to focus for longer periods will strengthen. Some days it will feel easier and other days almost impossible, even for a few seconds. That's fine. Keep going.

Making time to take care of your life

If you continually deny your need for self-care then you run the risk of burnout and ill-health. The expected response is 'I know that, but I don't have time.' There may well be very limited time for yourself so it's particularly important that you make good use of the time you do have. Some of the practices can be done within minutes or seconds and can quickly lead to a psychological and physiological change within you. The difficult part is getting yourself to the point of recognizing that you're allowed to put aside time for yourself and that it is essential, not a luxury or weakness, if you are to live a balanced life. You know you need to do it, just as you know you're reading this book because you need to stop smoking, for whatever reason.

Having said that, there will often be a nagging thought in your head trying to persuade you that you don't have enough time, that it's only for weaklings or that it makes you feel guilty for taking a break. Acknowledge these thoughts, then put them aside and ensure you do something for yourself each day, no matter how small.

Think of taking time as you do brushing your teeth. You do it every day, twice a day, in order to have fresh breath and to preserve your teeth and gums. You take time for oral hygiene each day without questioning it, so you can do the same for your physical and psychological health.

We all have five minutes in a day to do something good for ourselves. If you don't then you have a problem.

Learning how to be kinder and more compassionate towards yourself can change your view of yourself for the better. This can be one aspect that helps you to stop smoking as it can increase your sense of self-worth as well as your belief in your ability to manage your cravings and stop smoking.

If you are pressed for time then download an app, such as *iMindfulness on the Go*, on to your phone and listen to it with headphones while you're on the train, a passenger in the car or even when sitting in the garden or at your desk.

- You may be far too critical of yourself.
- Taking part in self-care practices can increase your ability to think of your own needs and address them in a better way.

Part 4

Going forward

12

The dreaded weight-gain issue

Not everyone will gain weight when quitting smoking. There are two reasons people tend to put on weight after quitting.

1 The gain may be due to a slowing of your metabolism as nicotine is a stimulant.
2 The gain may be due to substituting food for cigarettes.

The issue of substituting is extremely important as people frequently use food to replace that feeling of oral gratification once got from having a cigarette in their mouth. However, the use of, or increased use of, drugs, alcohol and sex are also other ways that may be used to get pleasure to replace cigarettes. The obvious concern is that these can cause problems too. It's like saying 'I'm addicted to the sugar in fizzy drinks so I'll stop drinking them and eat cream doughnuts.'

Talking of sugar, you may want to eat more sugar and carbo-hydrates – which are broken down into sugar or glucose in the body – when you stop smoking. Part of this is because you think sugar will lift your mood and make you feel satisfied. Dopamine plays a role in reward and motivation behaviour, and it affects the brain processes that control movement, emotional response, the ability to experience pain and pleasure. When you stop smoking your dopamine levels need time to find a balance: initially smoking released dopamine, a feel-good chemical, but over time you needed more and more nicotine for your body to release the same amount of dopamine. When you're no longer smoking your body needs to relearn how and when to secrete a normal amount, and this takes time.

Changes in your body

Metabolic alterations can occur after quitting, so there is often an automatic 5–10 lbs/2.27–4.55 kg weight gain over the first year.[1,2] However, some people lose weight, and the long-term benefits of quitting far exceed the disadvantages of gaining weight. A moderate increase in your weight won't increase your risk of dying, but smoking will, no matter whether you smoke 10 or 100 cigarettes a day.

Nicotine is an appetite suppressant and it elevates your blood sugar levels and your blood fat levels so your body thinks it has eaten between meals when it hasn't.[3] It's also common for smokers to end a meal with a cigarette or sometimes even to end the meal prematurely in order to have a cigarette. This ending signal is no longer there so you may continue eating beyond the point you used to when you smoked. Even earlier in the day smokers may have tea or coffee and a cigarette for breakfast. Without the nicotine to quell your appetite, you may wake up and soon feel hungry. This is good as you can now have a decent breakfast instead of a cigarette, which means you're feeding your body and balancing your glucose levels rather than feeding your addiction.

You are more likely to gain weight if you are:

- already overweight;
- a heavy drinker or didn't drink at all;
- a heavy smoker.[4]

It's often helpful to try not to diet during the quitting process but rather to diet once you're past that initial stage and on the road to recovery. Having said that, some people bite the bullet and go on a healthy eating plan at the same time as stopping smoking, as a way of improving what they eat, keeping control over their potentially unhealthy food intake and bringing a new structure and mindset into their lives.

As you have already read, every cigarette contains 7,000 chemicals, many of which are toxic. Once you stop smoking, your body will need time to readjust. You can help it by taking better care of what you now put into it.

Get moving

Smoking also causes heart disease because your heart increases by 10–20 beats a minute after a cigarette, which is one reason why this repeatedly unnatural increase caused by smoking can damage your heart. What you now want to aim to do is to increase your heart rate in a healthy way through exercise.

Gentle exercise, to start, is a good way of reminding yourself why you want to stop smoking. Run up the stairs and you'll know this in seconds. The idea is to build up your exercise gradually but also to make it fun. Join a walking club, meet a friend and go for a walk or jog, get your old tennis racket out and join a rusty rackets class, go to a pilates class. The important thing is that you get moving, that you get your heart rate up more and more over time and that you enjoy yourself. If it's a sociable environment then there's a better chance that you'll go and that you'll stick with it. The same holds if you have restricted movement due to ill health, age or for any other reason. Join in with any activities you can, organize for someone to go for a walk with you around your garden, the park or even outside on the road for a few minutes. If you're chairbound then do special exercises designed for this as you'll be surprised at the effort they can take and their benefits. Movement, even when in pain, is far better than no movement.

You need to up your heart rate when exercising, so moderate-intensity aerobic activity is what you should aim for, but get there at a moderate pace. Being active around the house or shopping doesn't get your heart rate up enough over a sufficient period of time. Around 20 minutes a day of fast walking, doubles tennis, water aerobics, riding a bike with some hills and pushing a non-electric lawnmover are all ways of achieving the 150 minutes a week guideline.[5]

Get mobile and keep mobile, both in body and in mind. If you aren't convinced then perhaps these facts will make it more real. People who do regular activity have:[6]

- up to a 35 per cent lower risk of coronary heart disease and stroke
- up to a 50 per cent lower risk of Type 2 diabetes
- up to a 50 per cent lower risk of colon cancer
- up to a 20 per cent lower risk of breast cancer
- a 30 per cent lower risk of early death
- up to an 83 per cent lower risk of osteoarthritis
- up to a 68 per cent lower risk of hip fracture
- a 30 per cent lower risk of falls (among older adults)
- up to a 30 per cent lower risk of depression
- up to a 30 per cent lower risk of dementia.

Get busy

If you only focus on being deprived then you'll become despondent, demotivated and feel as if the whole thing is too much. It will make an enourmous difference if you get busy and distract yourself from being in the same situations all the time that you were in when you smoked. Go dancing, do voluntary work (even if you have a full-time job), garden, take up golf – just stay away from smokers who tempt you and from situations that act as triggers. Speak on the phone in a different room or do it standing. If you go to the pub as a social place then join in the quiz or go with a non-smoking friend so that you aren't tempted to go outside and join the smoking clan or to sit and dream of the pleasure of having a drink and a cigarette after work or on a warm afternoon on the weekend.

Sleep

The demands and attitudes of modern life seem to impinge on the number of hours of sleep people get. Sleep is fundamental to your health, and getting enough good quality sleep is critical for good health.

Poor or insufficient sleep affects your cognitive abilities and con-centration, your food intake (coffee and chocolate sound familiar?), your will to exercise, your ability to deal with stressful or demanding tasks, your mood, the secretion of cortisol, which affects your organs and your weight as well as eventually slowing down your metab-olism, your memory and recall and many other factors.

Sleep is a time for repair and renewal of your body, but it's not only physical. Psychologically, when you're asleep your mind processes the events of the day and it works to allow pieces of infor-mation to be sorted and stored at a concious and unconscious level.

Sleep is also when you have time out from the activities of the day, the demands placed on you and the ongoing stimulation of people, phones, computers, radios and the general busyness around you, even in a quiet setting.

Watch your stress levels

Stress can make you fat, wear down your organs and act as a major trigger to relapsing. You'll have read about the effects of stress in Chapter 5, so you know that stress sets up a chain reaction in your body and that it can affect your weight, especially around your waist. This is very unhealthy as it puts pressure on your heart. Stress doesn't only affect your body but your emotional state and psychological health as well.

Ask for support

When trying to quit smoking, giving up, lower mood, anxiety, restlessness, increased use of drugs, sex or alcohol and other things are not uncommon, and it will make a difference if you ask for support or at least speak to people close to you or to professionals. Letting others know how you feel, what is happening inside you and what may help makes a difference to you and to them. There are many ways you can do this, some of which are anonymous, such as helplines. It doesn't help feeling guilty or ashamed as those emotions only pull you down. The necessary component needed is a willingness to speak, to ask and to negotiate what's needed. Quitting, if you're serious about it, is a whole new game; learning the rules takes time and practice.

Whole-person attitude

When you take on board that your mind and body work as one unit, that your thoughts, emotions and unconscious needs trigger physiological reponses in your body, such as releasing cortisol, and that your physical activities and behaviours activate psychological responses, then you recognize the importance of approaching your life and lifestyle from a wider and all-inclusive perspective.

The more responsible you are for all aspects of yourself and the more you work with each part (physical, emotional and psychological), the more integrated your life becomes, and that is part of what mindfulness can help you to know and maintain. There's no difference between not taking care of your most prized car that serves you in many ways and not taking care of yourself. You wouldn't run your petrol car on diesel or never service it, even when there's smoke billowing out of the engine. You know that it will either break down or blow up or do something that will mean you'll no longer have a car because you neglected it. The same goes for your body, and your life.

- Remember that you are a series of interconnected systems functioning as one unit.
- Think about all aspects of your lifestyle when you stop smoking.

13

Staying committed

Without commitment there will be no long-term progress. This is a challenge. To be able to increase your chances of stopping smoking, you will need to set boundaries to ensure you make time to do the practices and constantly come back to the mindset of mindfulness and not smoking.

Boundaries

As with any addiction, people make many excuses for their smoking habit: 'I'm too stressed', 'I'm overworked', 'It's the only thing that helps me relax', 'I really enjoy it.' And they avoid stopping with 'It's not the right time', 'I'll take my chances', 'I could get run over by a bus tomorrow.' When trying to change and commit to something new, such as mindfulness, excuses can arise too, such as 'I have no time', 'I can't focus' or 'I'm not doing silly stuff like that.' It's true that many have responsibilities in life – such as careers or families or both – that take up time and effort, but the only way you can make progress is if you set your mind to it. Don't forget: you find time to smoke, so you can use that time to meditate or think about your current mindset towards smoking.

> You need to ask yourself: 'What is so unimportant about my life that I won't give it any time?'

It may be tempting to view the mindfulness practices as another chore to tick off the list, but this isn't helpful. Instead you can see them as a time that is for you and you alone. There's no precise way to approach mindfulness but, undoubtedly, the more you do the practices the more they'll help. Finding the practices that work best for you will help you get the most out of mindfulness. However, as previously mentioned, it's not only about the formal practices, which are essential, but also about how you integrate the concepts and attitude into your life and way of being.

Releasing the grip

- Take a moment to focus on something in your life that is a source of suffering or stress. Perhaps it's one reason why you smoke. You may not have had the opportunity to fully acknowledge what it is and where it's come from. It may feel like a big knot in your mind or like a hand that's tightly clenched, unwilling to open. Over a period of time you can lock your negativity into a dark place in your mind where it can't be found.

- Focus on all the distress it causes you, whether it be mental or physical. Does it really deserve to take so much out of you? Try to soften your view of it. Do not give it attention or power, simply let it be and gently allow its grip to soften by breathing into it.

- There may also be good experiences you've had when smoking that reinforce your need to smoke. For example, you may have smoked when socializing and having a good time at a party. The hold these experiences have over you needs to be loosened as they can make you see smoking as a positive behaviour. Separate in your mind that it's not only the smoking that's enjoyable but also the company and camaraderie around it. Consequently, it will be important for you to find this sense of camaraderie or company somewhere else, otherwise you'll want to seek it out with smokers and increase your chance of relapsing.

- Let the imaginary clenched grip slowly open, releasing the power it holds by breathing into the image, letting its grip ease with each breath.

- Setting boundaries to do the practices increases your chances of long-term progress.
- The practices should not be seen as a chore but as a time of quiet and freedom for yourself.

14

Challenges to recovery

Your greatest challenge to recovery can be yourself. Challenges can come from a range of different angles: a lack of belief, a stubbornness to change, a laziness to commit. That's why taking responsibility for your life and your addiction is so important. Mindfulness, combined with the self-knowledge you developed from working with Tables 3 and 4 in Chapter 7, can be a route to greater awareness and acceptance.

Resistance

Being resistant to doing the practices, particularly in the early stages, is common. However, every time you focus and refocus your attention back to mindfulness and the practices it offers, you develop another strand of resilience. An additional challenge that may arise is staying with an emotion or thought that you experience during a practice. For instance, you may experience feelings of regret, frustration or shame over your smoking addiction or something else, or perhaps you are reminded of unsuccessful attempts to quit smoking in the past. It may feel easier to push these thoughts away rather than continue to stay with them. However, observing what thoughts come to consciousness and letting them be there without reacting to, or judging, them will help you to move forward.[1]

After a while you may be tempted to stop doing the practices or to stop this altogether because it's not working in the way you'd hoped.

This is fine; it's about making a choice as to whether or not to continue and then deciding, if you want to continue, which practices are the most useful for you as an individual. Remember that coming in with the expectation that mindfulness will solve all your problems will only lead to disappointment. However, with commitment it can help you to become more aware of how best to deal with and manage yourself and your cravings from day to day.

Your internal barrier

The other challenge is allowing yourself the chance to try it without dismissing it as quackery or nonsense. This is a barrier, a defence against recognizing that if you really want to stop, then you'll do whatever it takes, no matter how difficult it is. People do stop smoking, and do so forever, by learning how to manage their triggers and cravings and by shifting their mindset. It's about putting one foot in front of the other. No great leaps or jumping from dizzy heights: it's about pacing and constantly negotiating with yourself. If you're craving, use the **I-QUIT** steps and tell yourself that it is for this moment – and for this moment and each new moment that follows. You'll know of the 'one day at a time' idea. That's often too long a period for smokers, so break it down into one hour or the next five minutes, even saying 'For this moment, I won't smoke and I'll see how I feel after that.' Make it manageable, because just like thoughts and intense feelings, cravings too will pass.

Now is not forever but now + now + now will get you one moment at a time to forever – and to forever not smoking.

There is no end-point with mindfulness. From one day to the next, each moment presents a new chance to recognize and react differently to your thoughts and feelings and to your cravings and reactions.

- Mindfulness is not a short or easy process; there are a range of challenges that can arise and that should be dealt with appropriately.
- Discovering which practices work best for you is part of what it's all about.

15

Reap the rewards

If you remain committed and motivated to progress with mindfulness in the coming weeks and months, you will start to become aware of the rewards it brings and will notice a change in your outlook. These changes will aid your awareness of why and when you smoke and help you to rely less on smoking as a comforting or pleasurable habit or reaction. You will begin to realize that there are other options available that are far healthier and more beneficial for you.

To see more clearly what mindfulness is bringing you, here are some points for you to think about, and keep track of, on a regular basis.

- In which situations does being mindful most benefit you?
- Identify one time and place that you practise mindfulness each day, if only for five minutes.
- Which mindfulness practices are you finding most useful in relation to your smoking habit, and why?
- What are the most important or surprising aspects that you have learnt about yourself or your smoking habit since starting the mindfulness practices?
- What physical and psychological/emotional changes has mindfulness brought you?
- Which strategies will you use to ensure you continue to practise mindfulness long term?

Practising mindfulness will develop within you an ever-growing reserve to help you manage your smoking habit as well as life's experiences now and over the years to come. It most certainly also encourages and develops your ability to enjoy the good in life more fully. As mentioned earlier, it's not a quick fix and it may be a bumpy road at times, but if you commit to it, mindfulness will make you a stronger, more grounded individual, with greater control over your thoughts, emotions and responses.[1]

Think of mindfulness as a shoulder to lean on. It's dependable and it can create a real sense of stability, protection and balance that you may have struggled to find in the past. It can help you to move forward in order to stop smoking and to achieve whatever it is you want to achieve.

You are your responsibility, so it is up to you how you take care of yourself and what decisions you take. No one else is responsible for you except you.

With time you will see the rewards that mindfulness can bring you. It can help bring awareness to your life and how your smoking fits into it. Mindfulness will provide you with a form of resilience and self-protection that will strengthen and balance you.

Finally, remember that every day with mindfulness, every practice completed and every resisted craving is a step forward and a step towards a life without smoking. Mindfulness changes your brain and your mindset, your attitude towards yourself and your approach to life, so the more you do it the greater its benefits in so many areas of your life. You can change your life forever.

Quit smoking one breath at a time and change your life forever.

Notes

Introduction

1 US Department of Health and Human Services (2010), *How Tobacco Smoke Causes Disease: What It Means to You*, Atlanta, GA: US Department of Health and Human Services, Centers for Disease Control and Prevention, National Center for Chronic Disease Prevention and Health Promotion, Office on Smoking and Health.

1 Why do I smoke?

1 Wald, N. and Nicolaides-Bouman, A. (1991), *UK Smoking Statistics*, Oxford: Oxford University Press.

2 Somov, P. G. and Somova, M. J. (2011), *The Smoke-Free Smoke Break: Stop Smoking Now with Mindfulness and Acceptance*, Oakland, CA: New Harbinger.

3 American Cancer Society – <http://mcancer.org>.

4 <www.cancerresearch.co.uk>.

5 <www.cancerresearch.co.uk/tobacco>.

6 US Department of Health and Human Services – <www.cdctobaccofree.com>.

7 <www.cancerresearch.co.uk/tobacco>.

8 Mokdad, A. H., Marks, J. S., Stroup, D. F. and Gerberding J. L. (2004), 'Actual Causes of Death in the United States'. *JAMA, Journal of the American Medical Association* 291(10), pp. 1238–45.

9 <www.cancerresearch.co.uk>.

10 <www.healthline.com/smokingcessation/effects-of-smoking>.

11 <www.cancerresearch.co.uk>.

12 United States of America Centers for Disease Control and Prevention (CDC) – <www.cdc.gov/tobacco/about>.

13 American Cancer Society – <www.mcancer.org>.

14 Mental Health Foundation – <www.mentalhealth.org.uk/help-information/mental-health-a-z/s/smoking>.

15 Paperwalla, K. N., Levin, T. T., Weiner, J. and Saravay, S. M. (2004), 'Smoking and Depression', *Medical Clinics of North America* 88(6), pp. 1483–94.

16 National Institute on Drug Abuse, USA.

17 Paperwalla et al., 'Smoking and depression'.

18 Paperwalla et al., 'Smoking and depression'.

19 Boden, J. M., Fergusson, D. M. and Horwood, L. J. (2010), 'Cigarette Smoking and Depression: Tests of Causal Linkages Using Longitudinal Birth Cohort', *British Journal of Psychiatry* 196(6), pp. 440–6.

20 Glassman, A. H., Helzer, J. E., Covey, L. S., Cottler, L. B., Steiner, F., Tipp, J. E. and Johnson, J. (1990), 'Smoking, Smoking Cessation, and Major Depression', *JAMA* 264(12), pp. 1546–9.

21 Paperwalla et al., 'Smoking and depression'.

22 Boden et al., 'Cigarette Smoking and Depression'.

23 McDermott, M. S., Marteau, T. M., Hollands, G. J. and Aveyard, P. (2013), 'Change in Anxiety Following Successful and Unsuccessful Attempts at Smoking Cessation: Cohort Study', *British Journal of Psychiatry* 202(1), pp. 62–7.

24 Anda, R. F., Williamson, D. F., Escobedo, L. G., Mast, E. E., Giovino, G. A. and Remington, P. L. (1990), 'Depression and the Dynamics of Smoking: A National Perspective', *JAMA* 264(12), pp. 1541–5.

25 Schneider, N. G. and Houston, J. P. (1970) 'Smoking and Anxiety', *Psychological Reports* 26(3), pp. 941–2.

26 Mental Health Foundation, <www.mentalhealth.org.uk/help-information/mental-health-a-z/s/smoking>.

27 Mental Health Foundation, <www.mentalhealth.org.uk/help-information/mental-health-a-z/s/smoking>.

28 Pratt, L. A. and Brody, D. J. (2010), 'Depression and Smoking in the U.S. Household Population Age 20 and Over, 2005–2008', National Center for Health Statistics (NCHS) Data Brief No. 34.

29 Anda et al., 'Depression and the Dynamics of Smoking'.

30 Anda et al., 'Depression and the Dynamics of Smoking'.

31 Taylor, G., McNeill, A., Girling, A., Farley, A., Lindson-Hawley, N. and Aveyard, P. (2014), 'Change in Mental Health After Smoking Cessation: Systematic Review and Meta-analysis', *British Medical Journal* 348:g1151.

32 Chang, C.-K., Hayes, R. D., Perera, G., Broadbent, M. T. M., Fernandes, A. C., Lee, W. E., Hotopf, M. and Stewart, R. (2011), 'Life Expectancy at Birth for People with Serious Mental Illness and Other Major Disorders from a Secondary Mental Health Care Case Register in London' (2011), *PloS One* 6(5), e19590.

33 Windle, M. and Windle, R. (2001), 'Depressive Symptoms and Cigarette Smoking Among Middle Adolescents: Prospective Associations and

Intrapersonal and Interpersonal Influences', *Journal of Counselling and Clinical Psychology* 69(2), pp. 215–56.

34 Johnson, J. G., Cohen, P., Pine, D. S., Klein, D. F., Kasen, S. and Brook, J. S. (2000), 'Association Between Cigarette Smoking and Anxiety Disorders During Adolescence and Early Adulthood' *JAMA* 284(18), pp. 2348–51.

35 Taylor, G., McNeill, A., Girling, A., Farley, A., Lindson-Hawley, N. and Aveyard, P. (2014), 'Change in Mental Health after Smoking Cessation: Systematic Review and Meta-Analysis', *British Medical Journal* 348:g2216.

36 McDermott, M. S., Marteau, T. M., Hollands, G. J. and Aveyard, P. (2013), 'Change in Anxiety Following Successful and Unsuccessful Attempts at Smoking Cessation: Cohort Study', *British Journal of Psychiatry* 202(1), pp. 62–7.

37 NHS Choices. 'Stopping Smoking Is Good for Your Mental Health' – <www. nhs.uk/Livewell/smoking/Pages/stopping-smoking-benefits-mental-health. aspx>.

38 <http://betobaccofree.hhs.gov/health-effects/secondhand-smoke/index.html>.

39 <http://betobaccofree.hhs.gov/health-effects/smoking-health/index.html>.

40 US Department of Health and Human Services (2010), *How Tobacco Smoke Causes Disease: What It Means to You*, Atlanta, GA: US Department of Health and Human Services, Centers for Disease Control and Prevention, National Center for Chronic Disease Prevention and Health Promotion, Office on Smoking and Health.

2 What is mindfulness?

1 Rezek, C. A. (2012), *Brilliant Mindfulness: How a Mindful Approach Can Help You Towards a Better Life*, Harlow: Pearson.

2 Allen, N., Chambers, R., Knight, W., Blashki, G., Ciechomski, L., Hassed, C., Gullone, E., McNab, C. and Meadows, G. (2006), 'Mindfulness-based Psychotherapies: A Review of Conceptual Foundations, Empirical Evidence and Practical Considerations', *Australian and New Zealand Journal of Psychiatry* 40(4), pp. 285–94.

3 McBee, L. (2003), 'Mindfulness Practice with the Frail Elderly and Their Caregivers', *Topics in Geriatric Rehabilitation* 19(4), pp. 257–64.

4 The evidence

1 de Souza, I. C., de Barros, V. V., Gomide, H. P., Miranda, T. C., Kozasa, E. H. and Noto, A. R. (2015), 'Mindfulness-based Interventions for the Treatment of Smoking: A Systematic Literature Review', *Journal of Alternative Complementary Medicine* 21(3), pp. 129–40.

2 Libby, D. J., Worhunsky, P. D., Pilver, C. E. and Brewer, J. A. (2012), 'Meditation-induced Changes in High-frequency Heart Rate Variability Predict Smoking Outcomes', *Frontiers in Human Neuroscience* 6(54).

3 Nosen, E. and Woody, S. R. (2013), 'Brief Psycho-education Affects Circadian Variability in Nicotine Craving During Cessation', *Drug and Alcohol Dependence* 132(1–2), pp. 283–9.

4 Brewer, J. A., Mallik, S., Babuscio, T. A. et al. (2011), 'Mindfulness Training for Smoking Cessation: Results from a Randomized Controlled Trial', *Drug and Alcohol Dependence* 119(1–2), pp. 72–80.

5 Khanna, S. and Greeson, J. M. (2013), 'A Narrative Review of Yoga and Mindfulness as Complementary Therapies for Addiction', *Complementary Therapies in Medicine* 21(3), pp. 244–52.

6 Witkiewitz, K., Lustyk, M. K. and Bowen, S. (2013), 'Retraining the Addicted Brain: A Review of Hypothesized Neurobiological Mechanisms of Mindfulness-based Relapse Prevention', *Psychology of Addictive Behaviors* 27(2), pp. 351–65.

7 Parks, G. A., Anderson, B. K. and Marlatt, G. A. (2001), *Interpersonal Handbook of Alcohol Dependence and Problems*, New York: Wiley.

8 Davis, J. M., Mills, D. M., Stankevitz, K. A., Smith, S. S. (2013), 'Pilot Randomized Trial on Mindfulness Training for Smokers in Young Adult Binge Drinkers', *BMC Complementary and Alternative Medicine* 13(1), p. 215.

9 Singh, N. N., Lancioni, G. E., Winton, A. S. W. et al. (2011), 'Effects of a Mindfulness-based Smoking Cessation Program for an Adult with Mild Intellectual Disability', *Research in Developmental Disabilities* 32(3), pp. 1180–5.

10 Kelley, M. M., Latta, R. E. and Gimmestad, K. (2012), 'Acceptance and Mindfulness-based Tobacco Cessation Interventions for Individuals with Mental Health Disorders', *Journal of Dual Diagnosis* 8(2), pp. 89–98.

11 Adams, C., McVay, M., Stewart, D. Copeland, A. (2012), 'Mindfulness Ameliorates the Relationship Between Weight Concerns and Smoking Behaviour in Female Smokers: A Cross-sectional Investigation', *Mindfulness* 3(11), pp. 179–85.

12 Witkiewitz, K. and Bowen, S. (2010), 'Depression, Craving and Substance Use Following a Randomized Trial of Mindfulness-based Relapse Prevention', *Journal of Consulting and Clinical Psychology* 78(3), pp. 362–74.

13 Merkes, M.(2010), 'Mindfulness-based Stress Reduction for People with Chronic Disease', *Australian Journal of Primary Health* 16 (3), pp. 200–10.

14 Oberg, E. B., Rempe, M. and Bradley, R. (2013), 'Self-directed Mindfulness Training and Improvement in Blood Pressure, Migraine Frequency, and Quality of Life', *Global Advances in Health and Medicine* 2(2), pp. 20–5.

15 Cresswell, J. D., Myers, H. F., Cole, S. W. and Irwin, M. R. (2009), 'Mindfulness

Meditation Training Effects on CD4+T Lymphocytes in HIV-1 Infected Adults: A Small Randomized Controlled Trial', *Brain, Behavior and Immunity* 23(2), pp. 86–97.

16 Smith, W. B. et al. 2006, 'A Preliminary Study of the Effects of a Modified Mindfulness Intervention on Binge Eating', *Complementary Health Practice Review* 11(3), pp. 133–43.

17 Winbush, N. Y., Gross, C. R. and Kreitzer, M. J. (2007), 'The Effects of Mindfulness-based Stress Reduction on Sleep Disturbance: A Systematic Review', *Explore (NY)* 3(6), pp. 585–91.

18 Merkes, M. (2010), 'Mindfulness-based Stress Reduction for People with Chronic Disease', *Australian Journal of Primary Health* 16(3), pp. 200–10.

19 Carlson, L. E., Speca, M., Patel, K. D. and Goodey, E. (2003), 'Mindfulness-based Stress Reduction in Relation to Quality of Life, Mood, Symptoms of Stress, and Immune Parameters in Breast and Prostate Cancer Outpatients', *Psychosomatic Medicine* 65(4), pp. 571–81.

20 Baer, R. A., Smith, G. T., Hopkins, J., Kreitemeyer, J. and Toney, L. (2006), 'Using Self-Report Assessment Methods to Explore Facets of Mindfulness', *Assessment* 13(1), pp. 27–45.

21 Deyo, M., Wilson, K. A., Ong, J. and Koopman, C. (2009), 'Mindfulness and Rumination: Does Mindfulness Training Lead to Reductions in the Ruminative Thinking Associated with Depression?', *Explore (NY)* 5(5), pp. 265–71.

22 Davidson, R. J., Kabat-Zinn, J., Schumacher, J., Rosenkranz, M., Muller, D., Santorelli, S. F., Urbanowski F., Harrington A., Bonus K.and Sheridan, J. F. (2003), 'Alterations in Brain and Immune Function Produced by Mindfulness Meditation', *Psychosomatic Medicine* 65(4), pp. 564–70.

23 Tang, Y. Y., Ma, Y., Wang, J., Fan, Y., Feng, S., Lu, Q., Sui, D., Rothbart, M. K., Fan, M. and Posner, M. I . (2007), 'Short-term Meditation Training Improves Attention and Self-regulation', *Proceedings of the National Academy of Science* 104(43), pp. 17152–6.

24 Tirch, D. D. (2010), 'Mindfulness as a Context for the Cultivation of Compassion', *International Journal of Cognitive Therapy* 3(2), pp. 113–23.

25 Smith, A. (2004), 'Clinical Uses of Mindfulness Training for Older People', *Behavioural and Cognitive Psychotherapy* 32(4), pp. 423–30.

26 Mrazek, M. D., Franklin, M. S., Phillips, D. T., Baird, B. and Schooler, J. W. (2013), 'Mindfulness Training Improves Working Memory Capacity and GRE Performance While Reducing Mind Wandering', *Psychological Science* 24(5): pp. 776–81.

27 Holzel, B. K., Carmody, J., Vangel, M., Congleton, C., Yerramsetti, S. M., Gard, T. and Lazar, S. W. (2012, 'Mindfulness Practice Leads to Increases in Regional Gray Matter Density', *Psychiatry Research: Neuroimaging* 191(1), pp. 36–43.

28 Cordon, S. L. and Finney, S. J. (2008), 'Measurement Invariance of the Mindful Attention Awareness Scale across Adult Attachment Style', *Measurement and Evaluation in Counseling and Development* 40(4), pp. 228–45.

29 Carson, J. W., Carson, K. M., Gill, K. M. and Baucom, D. H. (2006), 'Mindfulness-based Relationship Enhancement (MBRE) in Couples', in R. A. Baer (ed.), *Mindfulness-based Treatment Approaches: Clinician's Guide to Evidence Base and Applications*, Burlington, MA: Elsevier, pp. 309–29.

30 Blake, C. (2010), *The Joy of Mindful Sex: Be in the Moment and Enrich Your Lovemaking*, Lewes: Ivy Press.

31 Pruitt, I. T. and McCollum, E. E. (2010), 'Voices of Experienced Meditators: The Impact of Meditation Practice on Intimate Relationships', *Contemporary Family Therapy* 32(2), pp. 135–54.

32 Chiesa, A. and Serretti, A. (2009), 'Mindfulness-based Stress Reduction for Stress Management in Healthy People: A Review and Meta-Analysis', *Journal of Alternative and Complementary Medicine* 15(5), pp. 593–600.

5 The stress response

1 Parrott, A. C. (1999), 'Does Cigarette Smoking Cause Stress?' *American Psychologist* 54(10), pp. 817–20.

6 The addiction

1 Royal College of Physicians and Royal College of Psychiatrists (2008), *Smoking and Mental Health*, London: Royal College of Physicians and Royal College of Psychiatrists.

2 National Institute on Drug Abuse, USA – <www.drugabuse.gov/publications/drugfacts/electronic-cigarettes-e-cigarettes>.

7 The bigger picture

1 Audrain-McGovern, J., Lerman, C., Wileyto, E. P., Rodriguez, D. and Shields, P. G. (2004), 'Interacting Effects of Genetic Predisposition and Depression on Adolescent Smoking Progression', *American Journal of Psychiatry* 161(7), pp. 1224–30.

2 Fergusson, D. M., Lynskey, M. T. and Horwood, L. J. (1995), 'The Role of Peer Affiliations, Social, Family and Individual Factors in Continuities in Cigarette Smoking Between Childhood and Adolescence', *Addiction* 90(5), pp. 647–59.

3 DeWit, D. J., MacDonald, K. and Offord, D. R. (1999), 'Childhood Stress and Symptoms of Drug Dependence in Adolescence and Early Adulthood', *American Journal of Orthopsychiatry* 69, pp. 61–72.

4 Rezek, C. A. (2010, *Life Happens: Waking up to Yourself and Your Life in a Mindful Way*, London: Leachcroft.

10 Stop and be mindful

1 Hayes, A. M. and Feldman, G. (2004), 'Clarifying the Construct of Mindfulness in the Context of Emotion Regulation and the Process of Change in Therapy', *Clinical Psychology: Science and Practice* 11(3), pp. 255–62.

11 Caring for yourself

1 Rezek, C. A. (2012), *Brilliant Mindfulness: How a Mindful Approach Can Help You Towards a Better Life*, Harlow: Pearson.

12 The dreaded weight-gain issue

1 Aubin, H., Farley, A., Lycett, D., Lahmek, P. and Aveyard, P. (2012), 'Weight Gain in Smokers after Quitting Cigarettes: Meta-analysis', *British Medical Journal* 345:e4439

2 <www.nhs.uk/Livewell/smoking/Pages/weightgain.aspx>.

3 <http://whyquit.com/joel/Joel_03_21_blood_sugar.html>.

4 <www.nhs.uk/Livewell/smoking/Pages/weightgain.aspx>.

5 <www.nhs.uk/conditions/stress-anxiety-depression/pages/stress-relief-exercise.aspx>.

6 <www.nhs.uk/conditions/stress-anxiety-depression/pages/stress-relief-exercise.aspx>.

14 Challenges to recovery

1 Peltz, L. A. (2013), *The Mindful Path to Addiction Recovery*, Boston, MA: Shambhala Publications.

15 Reap the rewards

1 Bowen, S., Chawla, N. and Marlatt, G. A. (2011), *Mindfulness-based Relapse Prevention for Addictive Behaviors*, New York: Guilford Press.